In My Father's House
Coloring Book

Shari S Lowell
Drawings: Wayne T. Sorenson
Contributors: Thomas Lowell,
Robert Lowell and Theodore Lowell

This book belongs to

_____

Introduction

My father, Wayne Sorenson, is a lot of things... he is a son, husband, father, Sunday School Superintendent, building designer, volunteer, mountain climber and artist. I have many amazing memories of growing up in the beauty of Everson, Washington and a lot of them are filled with images of watching my father sketching.

If you enter his work office, you will see walls covered with his pictures. You can't enter his car without removing a sketch pad from the car seats. There are always sketching materials next to his favorite chair, and when he isn't working on a building plan, you will find him at his drafting table with music on sketching away.

These pictures are mostly of historical homes, including places that no longer exist. Now that my father lives in Arizona, the buildings have an even more special meaning because they remind him of home. As he gets older and travels more, his home and office are filled with pictures of new places.

My father has always been interested not only in the buildings but also what goes on inside them. His pictures are often accompanied by photos and stories from the people who know the history of what has happened inside the walls.

It has always been a goal of mine to put together a coffee table book of all the homes designed by my father and call it "In My Father's House". That dream has been modified with input from my father to become this interactive coloring book. We have taken his original sketches and deconstructed them digitally removing some of the detail to allow the coloring artist to add their own imagination.

These are original pen and ink drawings that were sketched to be put behind glass and hung on a wall. It has been a great family project to turn them into this book and we hope you enjoy coloring the pages.

This book is dedicated to my family
Thomas, Robert and Theodore

And to my parents
Wayne and MaryAnn Sorenson

To my great grandparents:
Theodore and Belinda Sorenson
Who picked beautiful Everson as a homestead in 1905

And to all my other Sorenson relatives who keep Whatcom county as an inspiration for
their homes and for their art. Love to you all!

About the Artist and His Drawings - Wayne T Sorenson

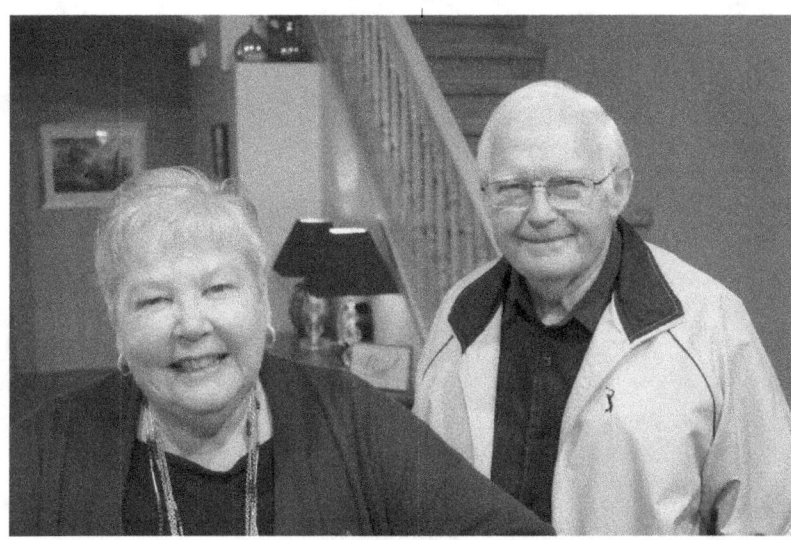

Wayne was born on November 5th, 1934 in Everson, Washington. He was raised on the family homestead on Sorenson Road in Whatcom County. He began sketching as a young child and sometimes got into trouble with teachers for drawing during school. However, Wayne's family and friends were delighted to see his sketches and they encouraged his early drawings. His interest began in elementary school, but has continued throughout his life. Wayne is self-taught, and has always enjoyed the freedom to draw what he found interesting and beautiful.

In his early twenties, Wayne served in the Army before pursuing a career as a building designer. He has had a career as a self-employed architect since 1960. Now at age eighty-two, Wayne is semi-retired, but still enjoys sketching at home as well as working on this new coloring book project.

Throughout his career, and still to this day, Wayne has sketched buildings as a hobby. His focus is on historic buildings and those with interesting characteristics. He has always tried to choose ones that reflect the personality of the community, owner, builder, and economic times. He has always been amazed by the tidbits of history related to each building. Wayne hopes that you will also find interest and beauty in the   pictures in this coloring book.

Wayne has been happily married to his wife, Maryann, since 1954, and they currently live in Sahuarita, Arizona. Their daughter Shari also resides in Sahuarita and their son Randy lives in Seattle, Washington. His latest endeavor has been to partner with his daughter Shari to create this coloring book. Wayne hopes that this book will allow you to find new beauty in his drawings as you personalize them and make them your own.

Tester Page

Place cardstock behind this page and test markers for color and for bleeding.
Cardstock in between pages will also help with pressure marks from pencils.

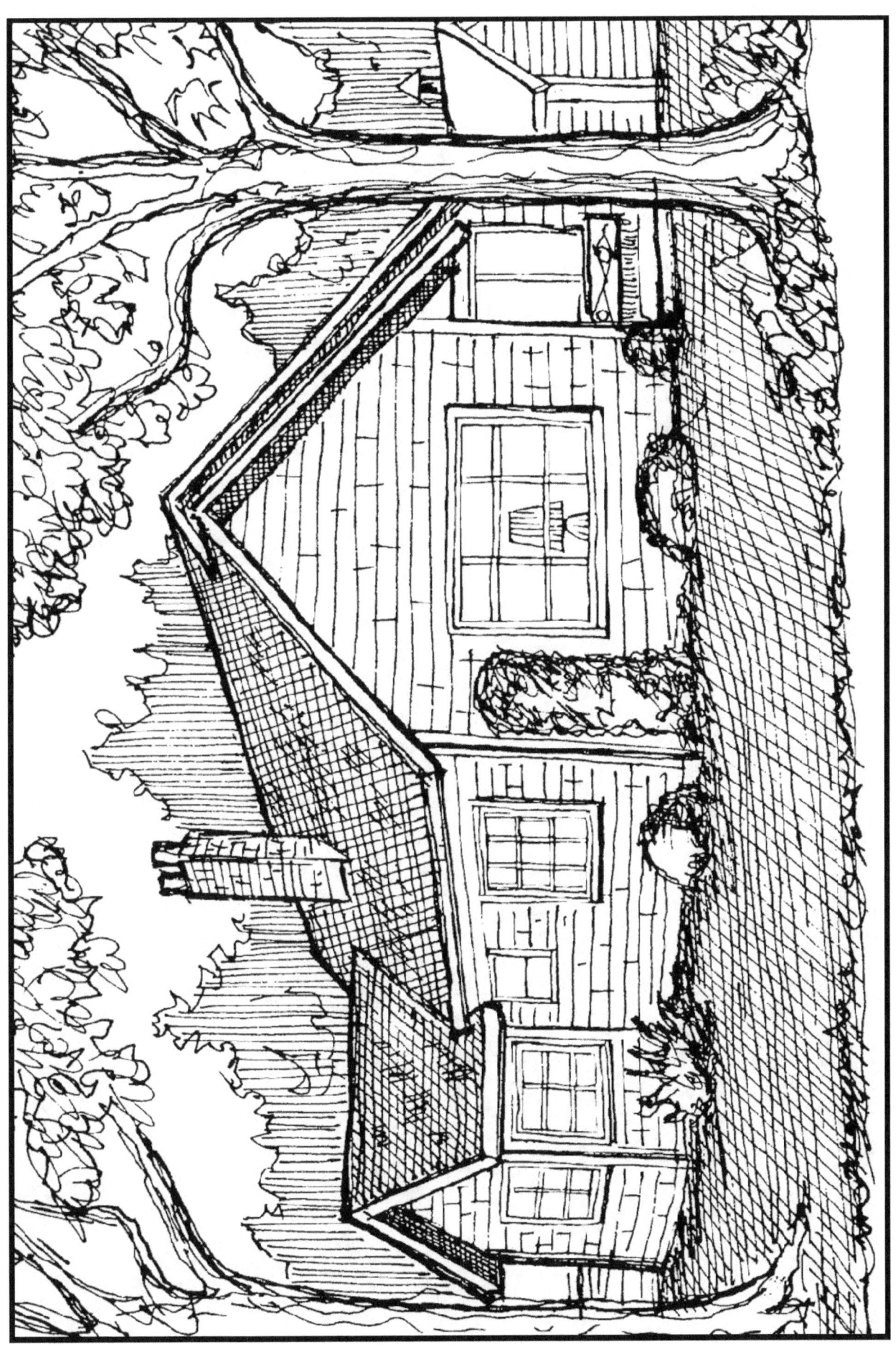

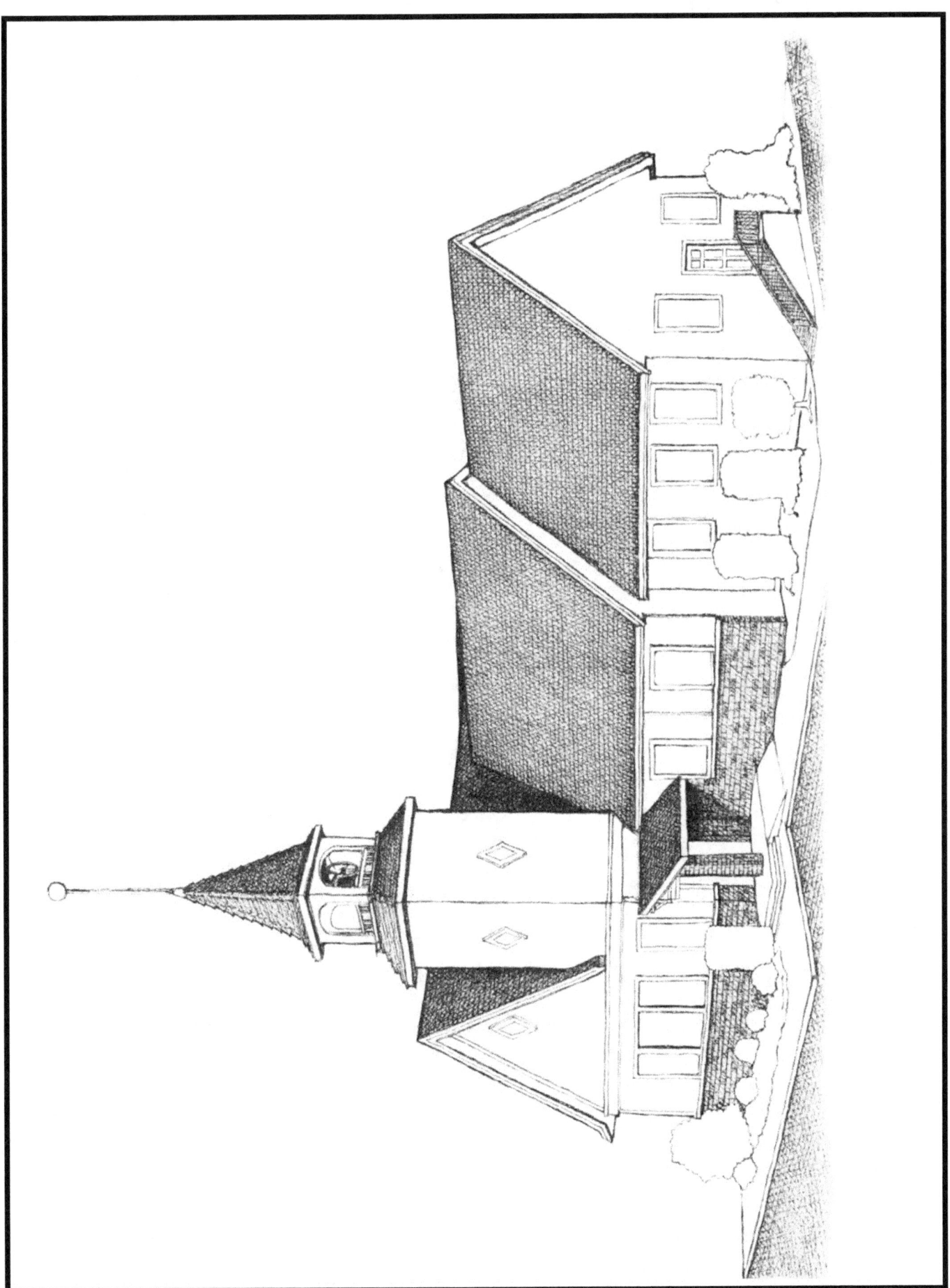

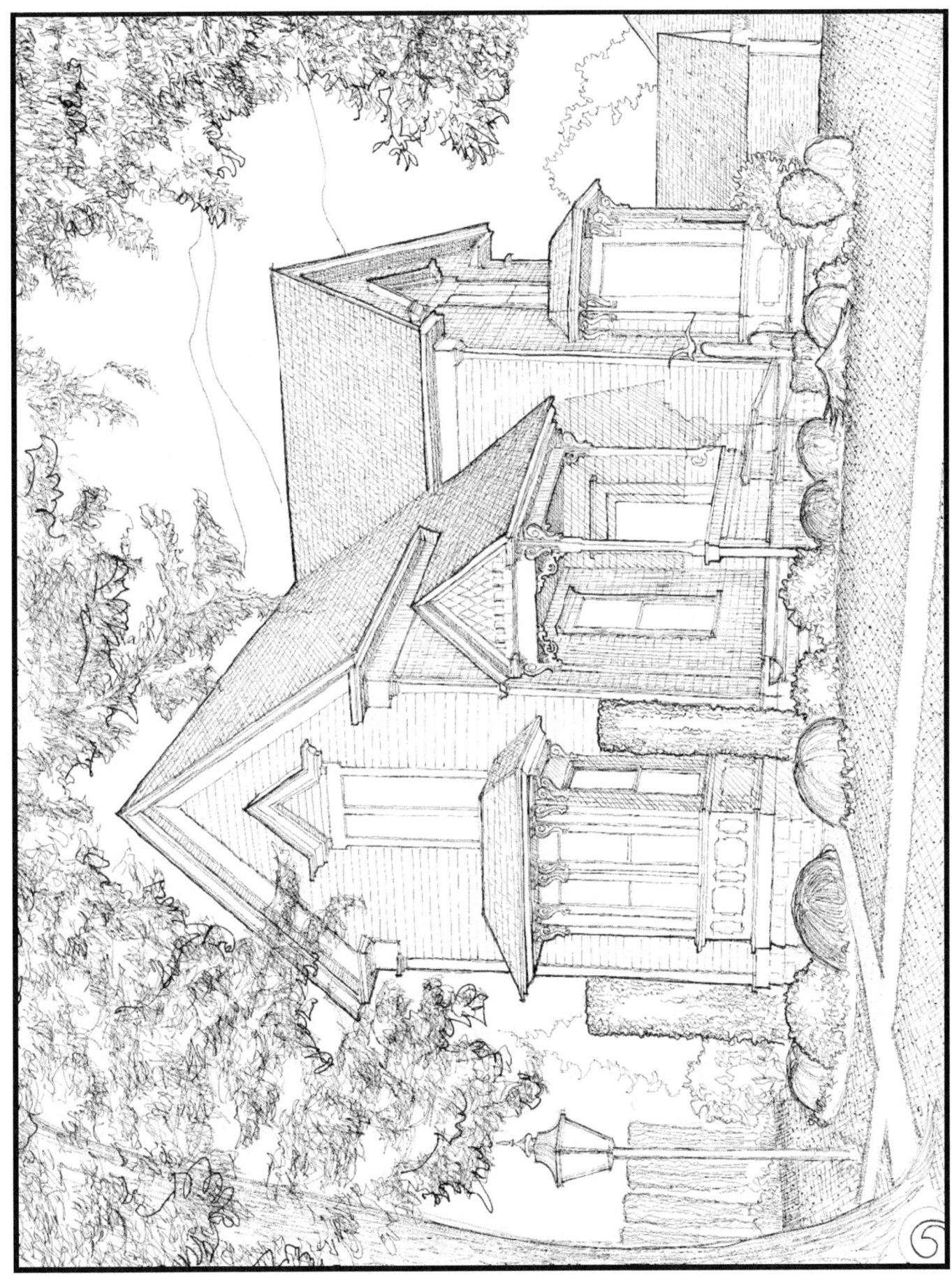

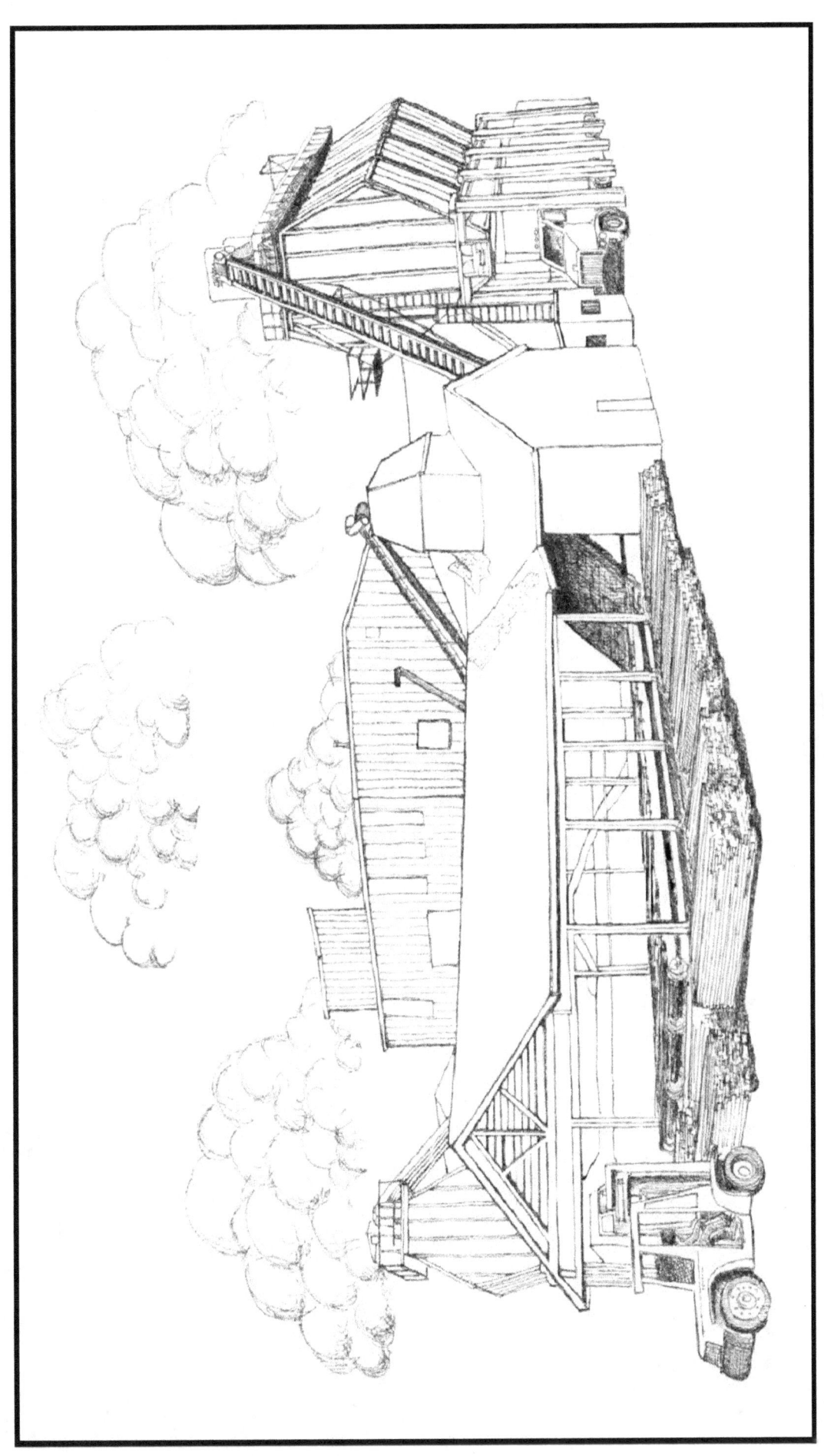

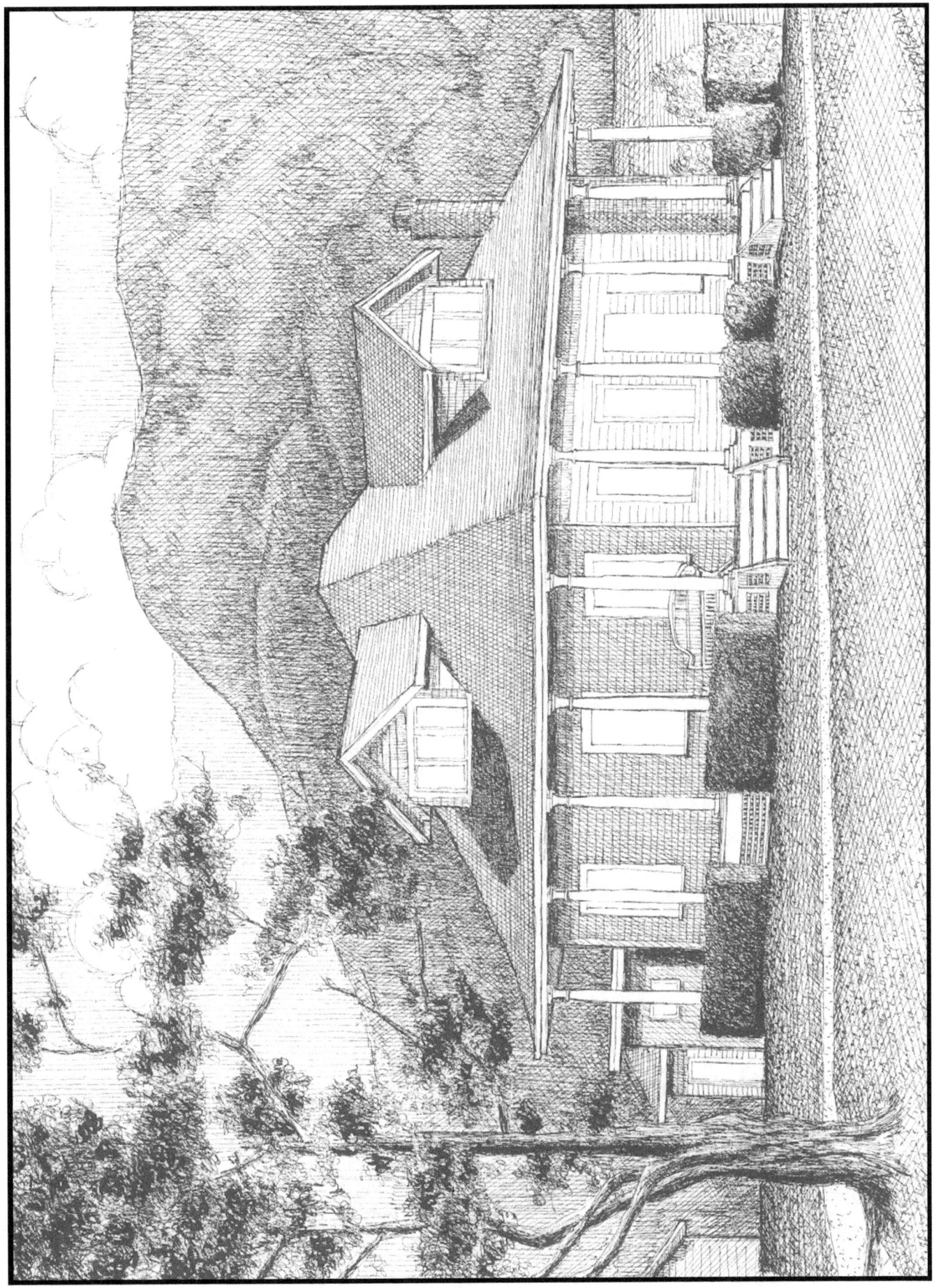

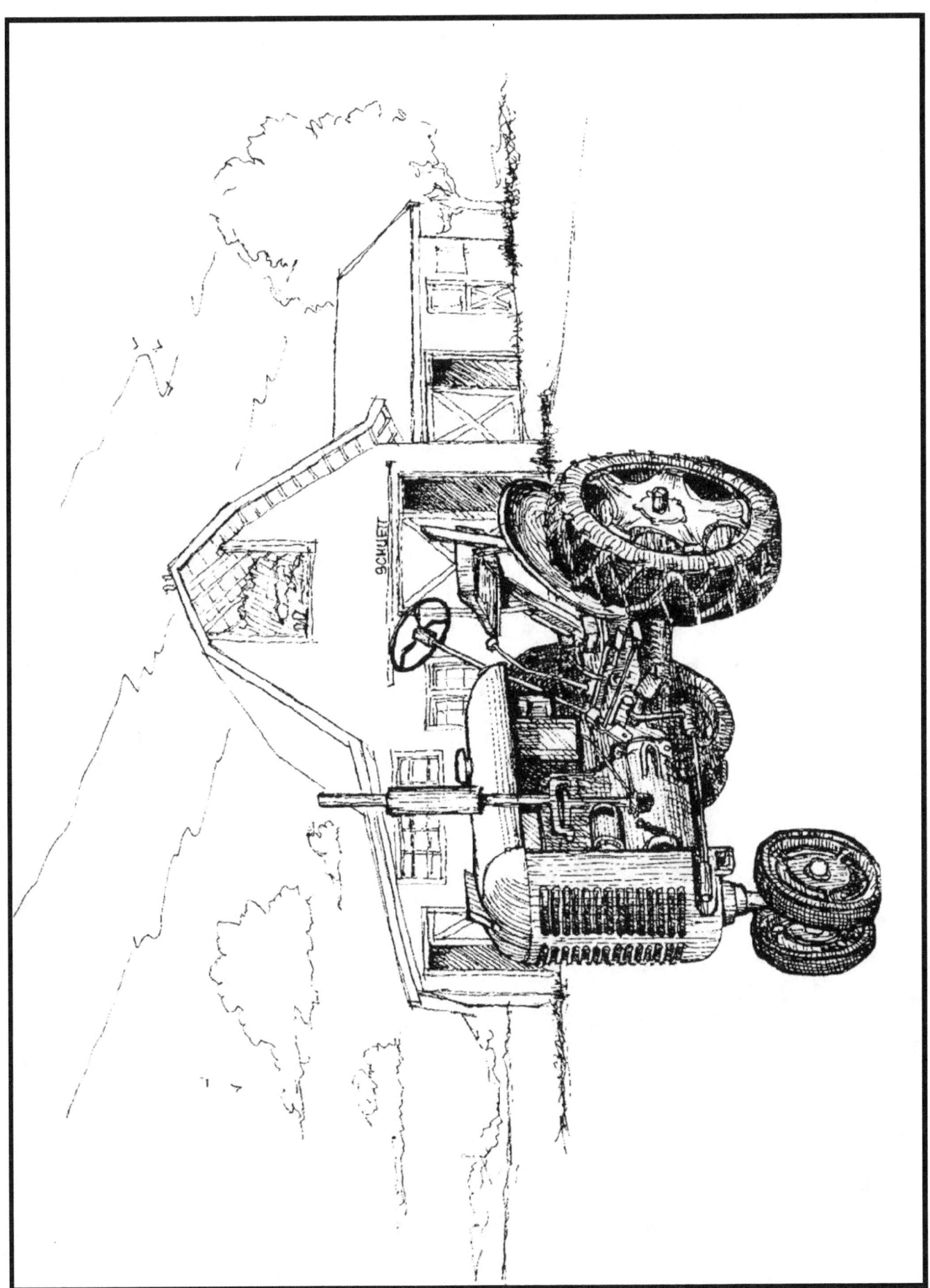

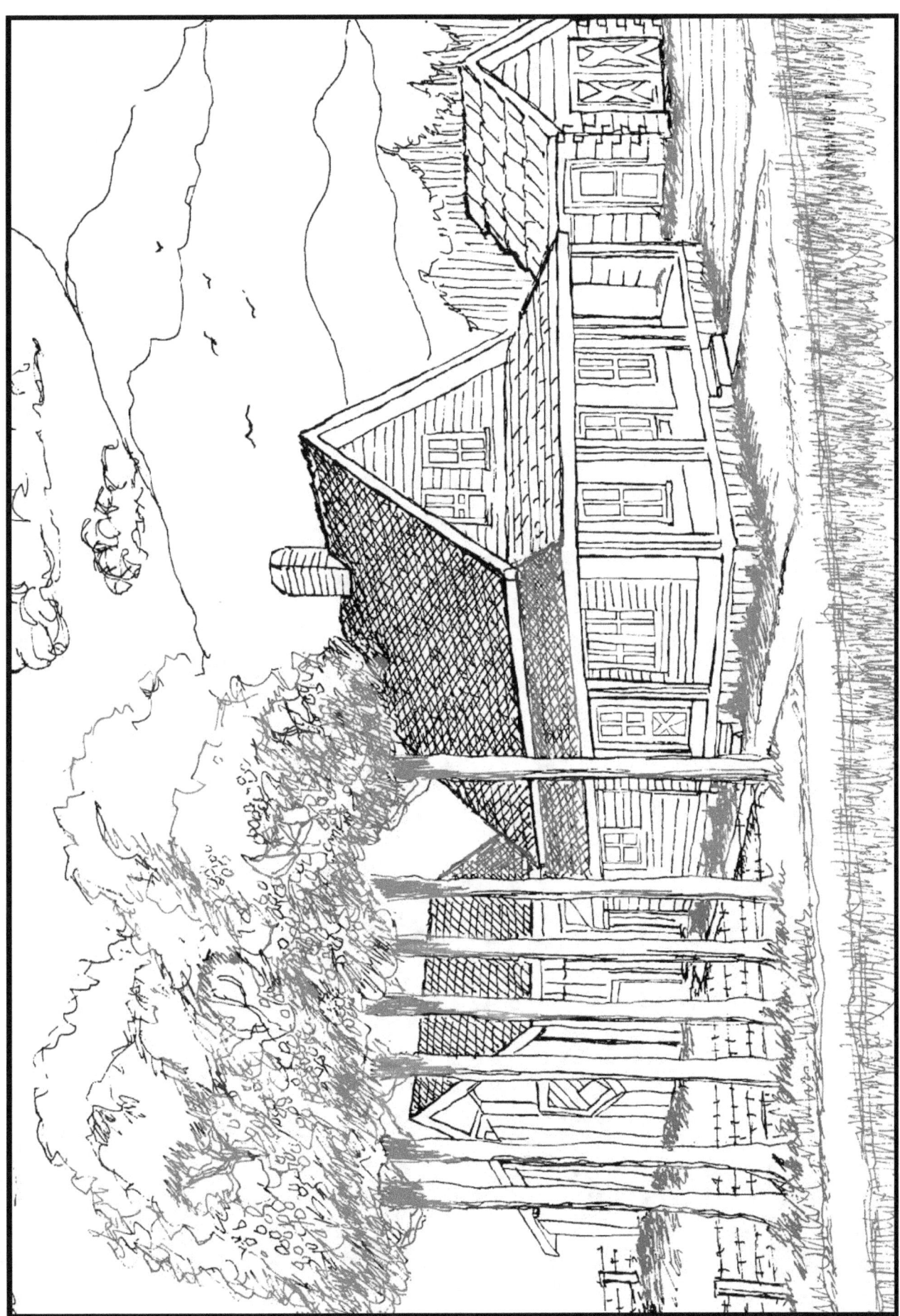

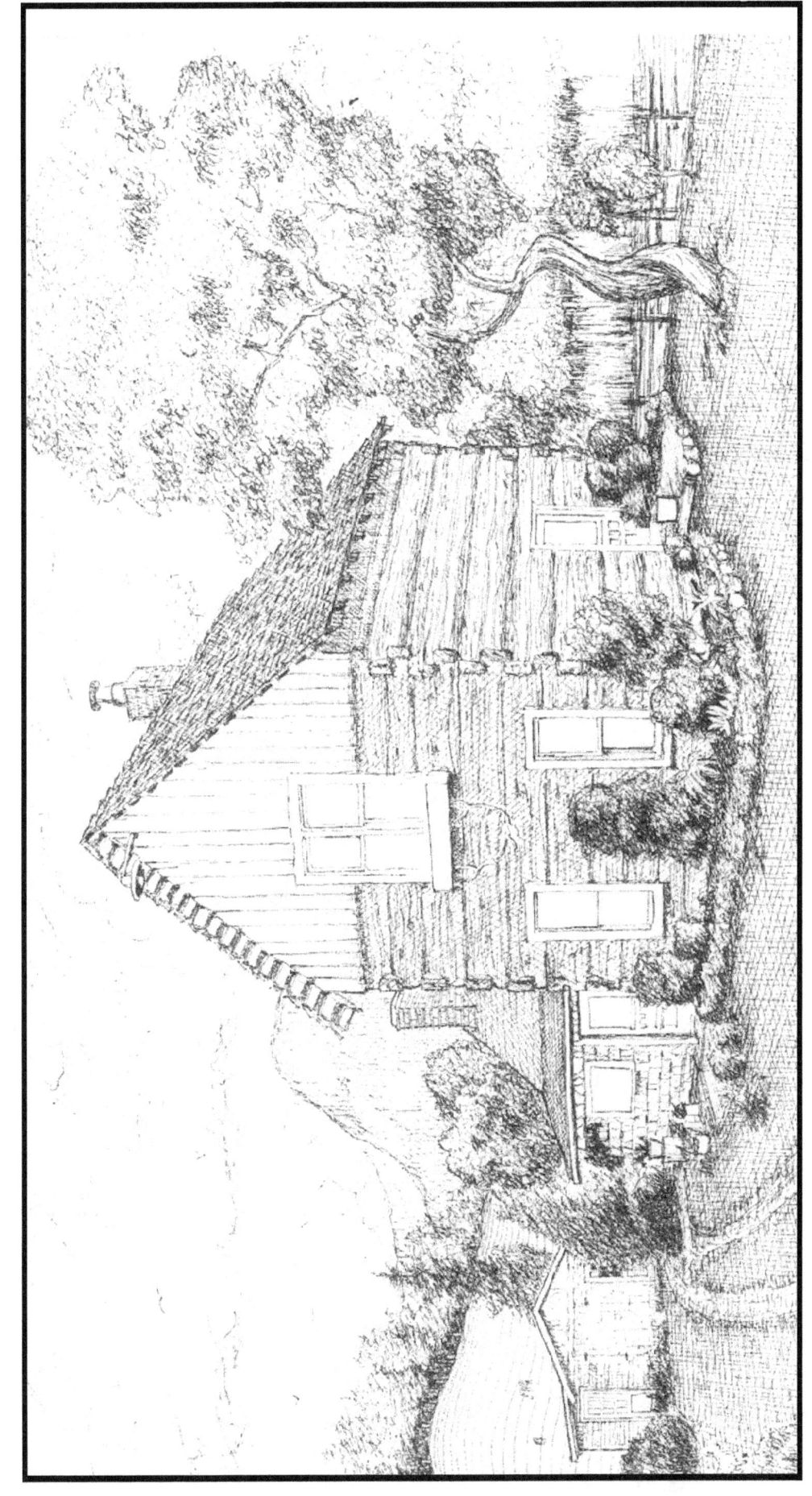

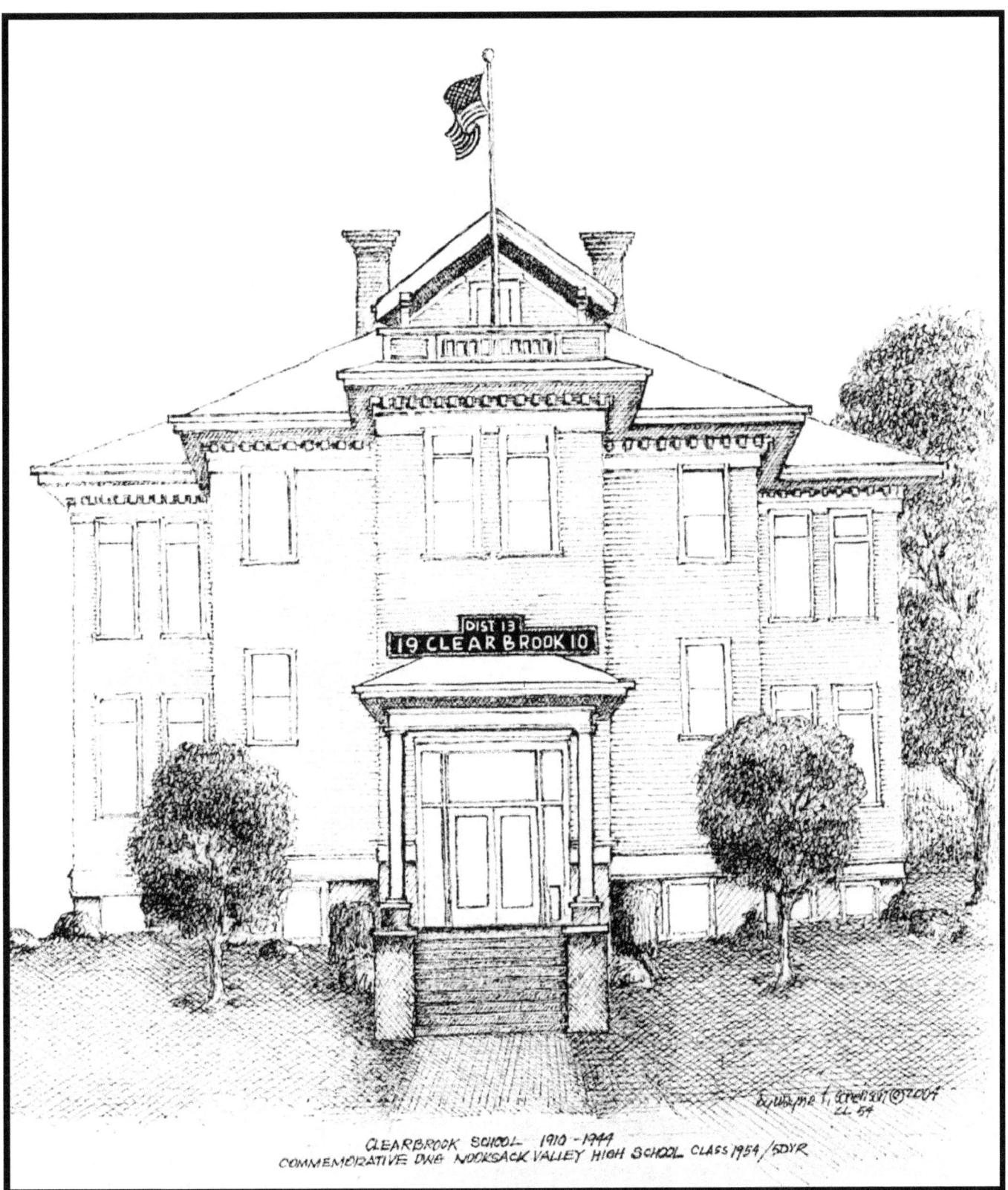

DIST 13
19 CLEARBROOK 10

CLEARBROOK SCHOOL 1910 - 1944
COMMEMORATIVE DWG NOOKSACK VALLEY HIGH SCHOOL CLASS 1954/5DYR

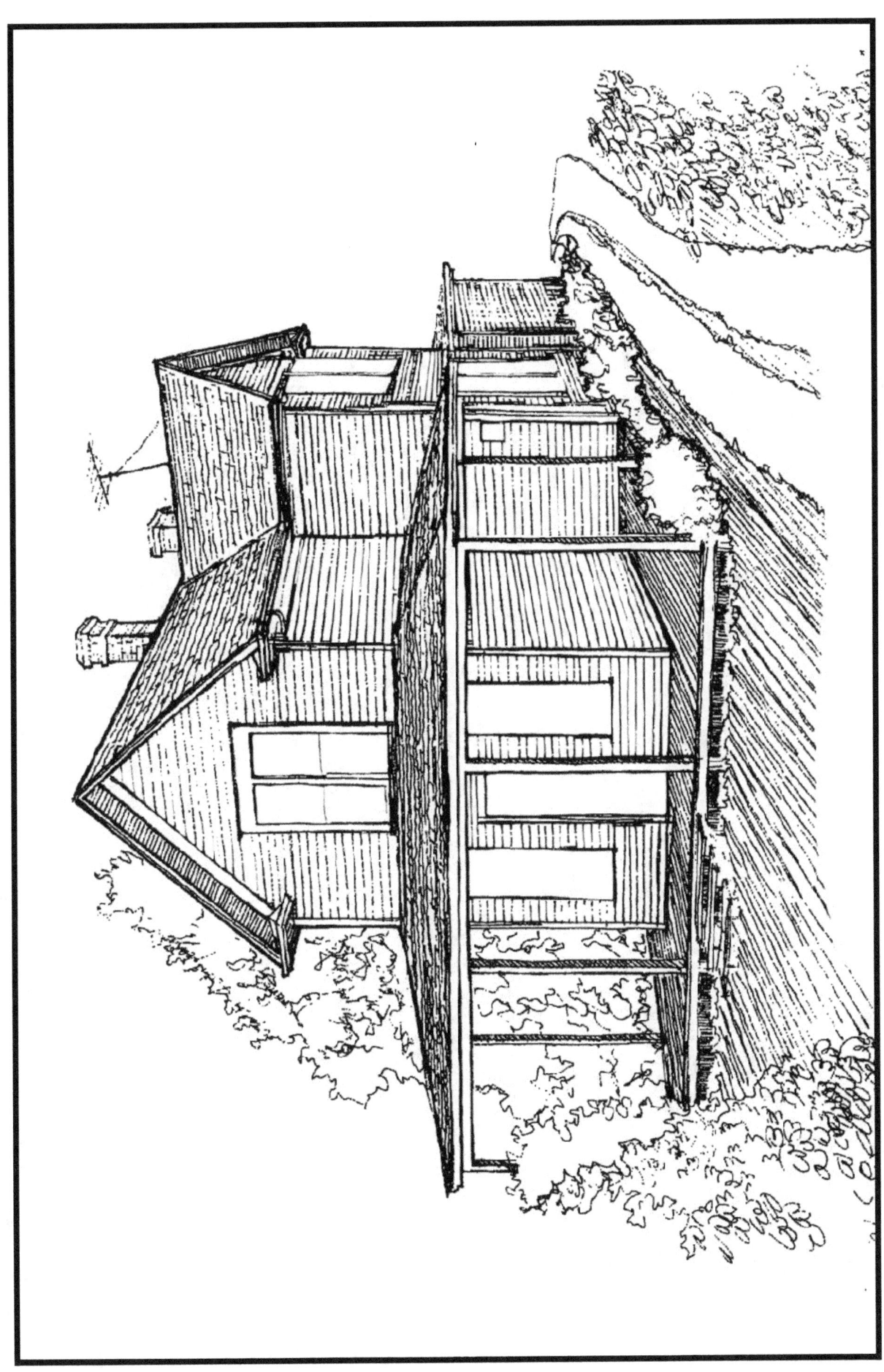

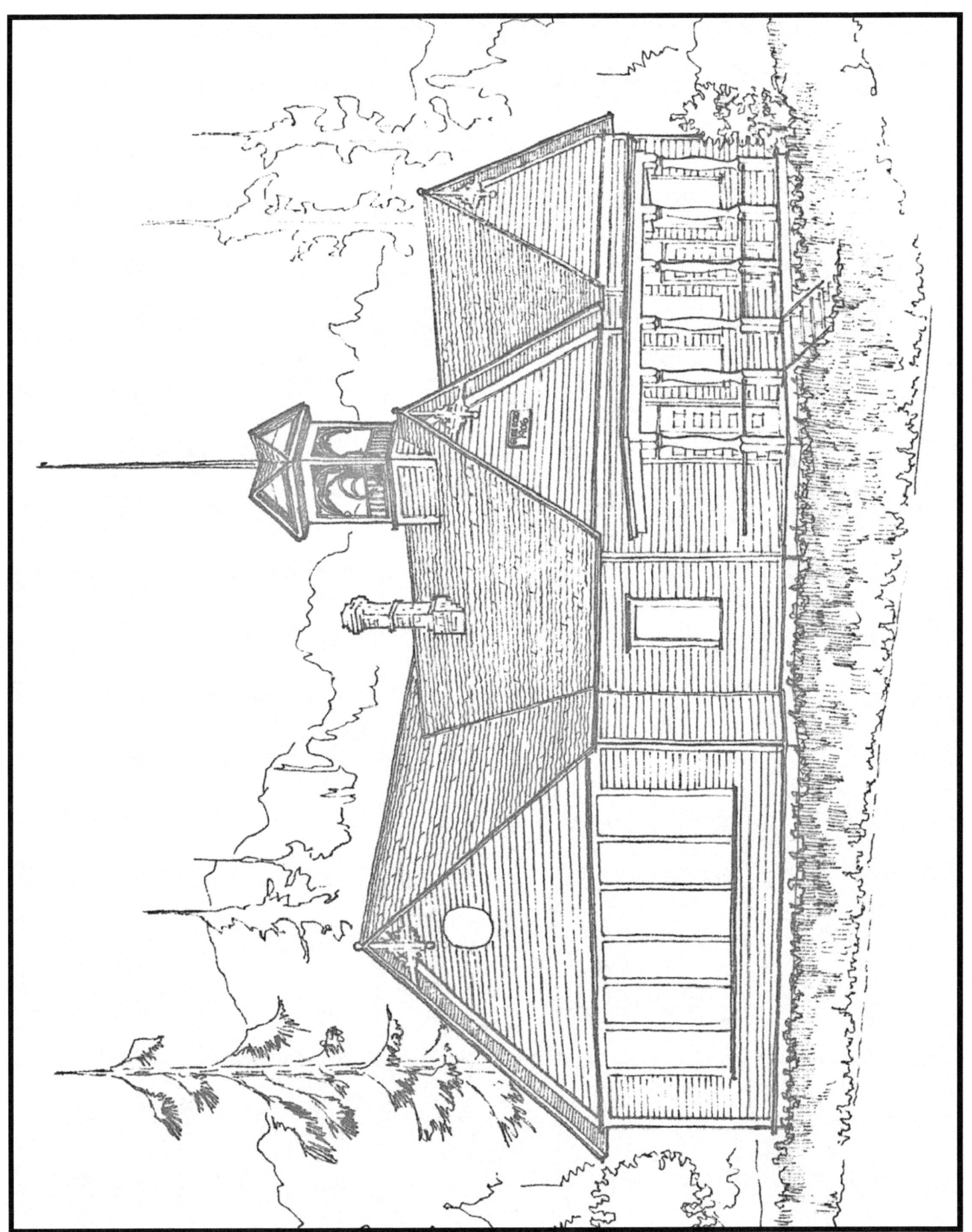

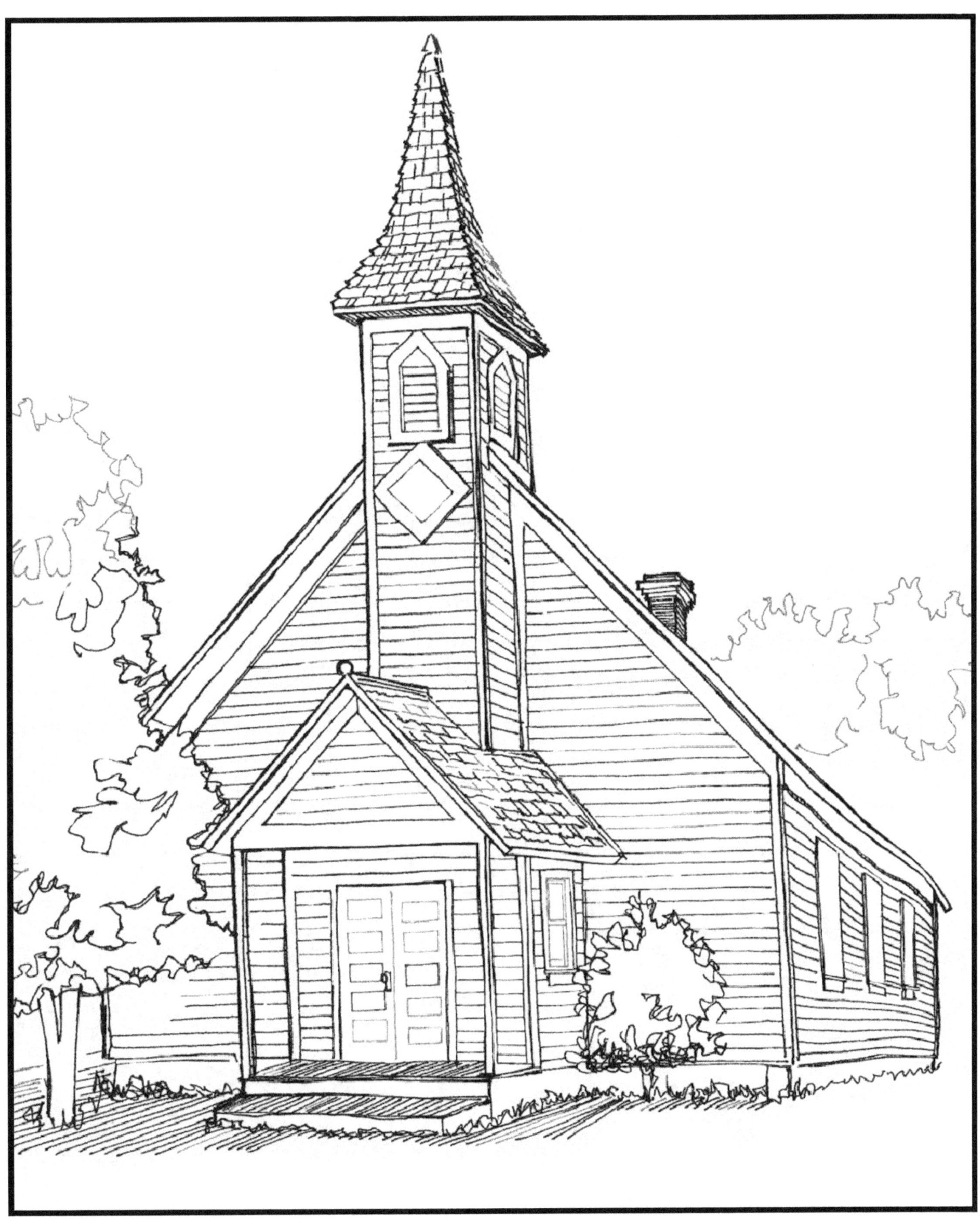

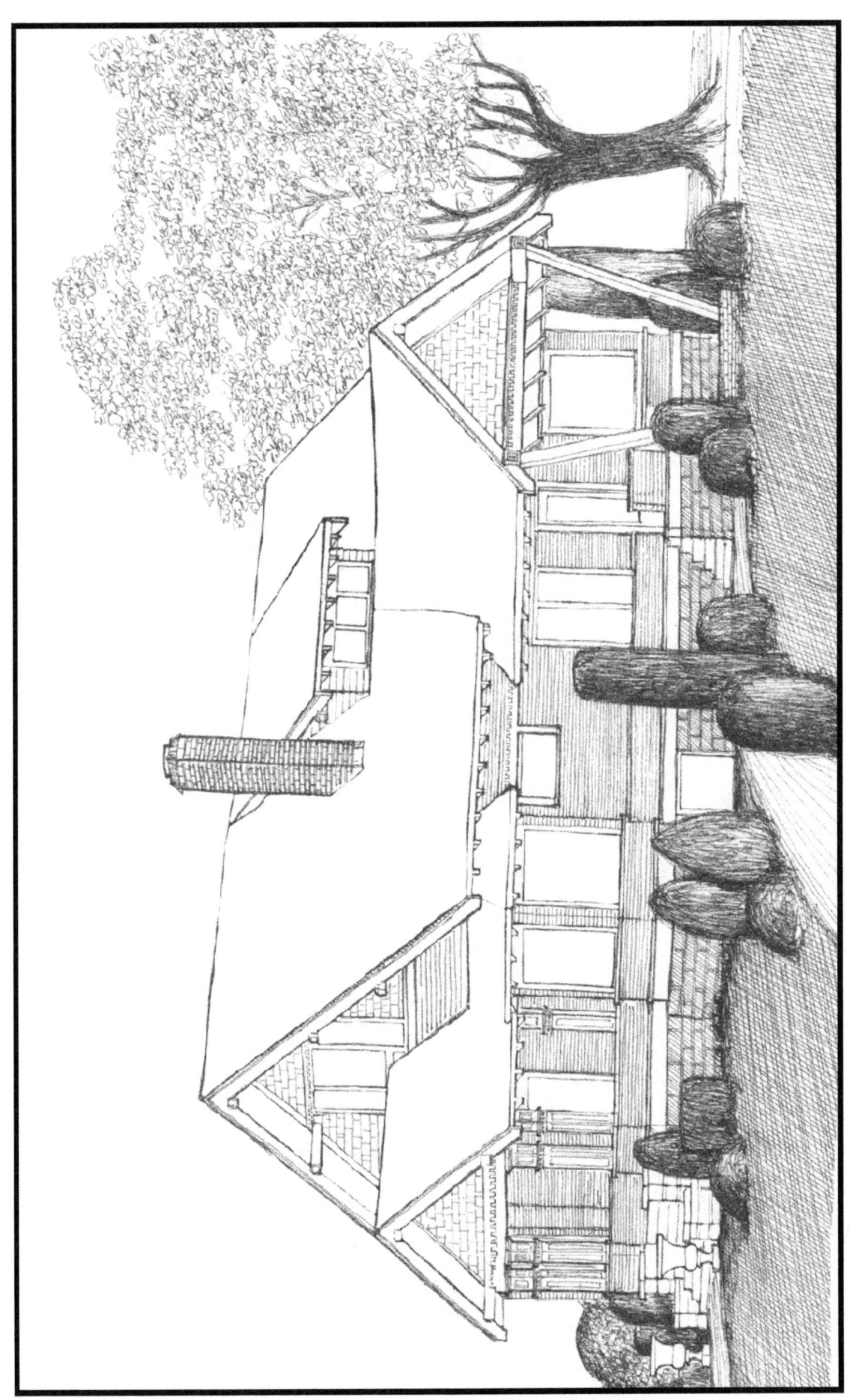

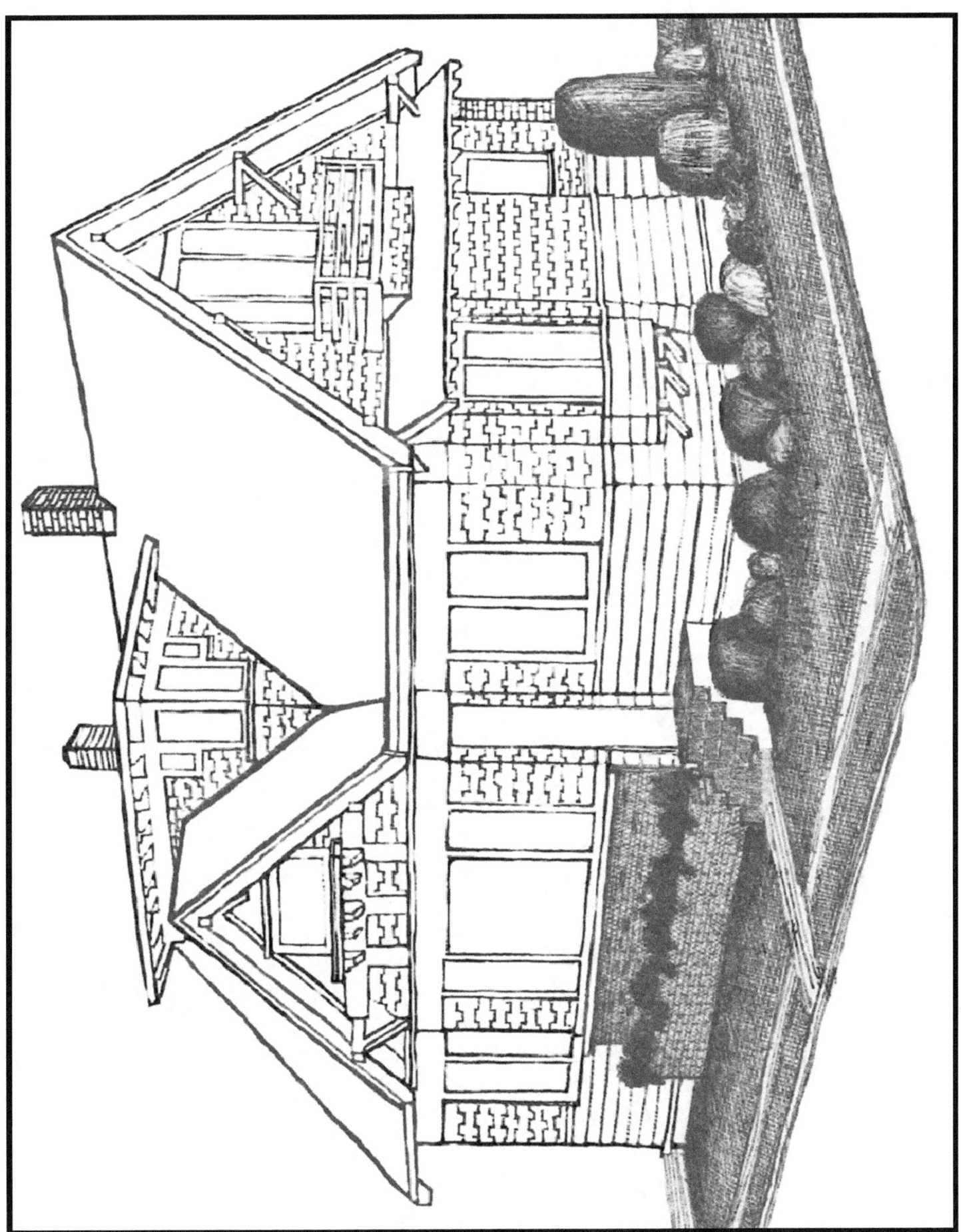

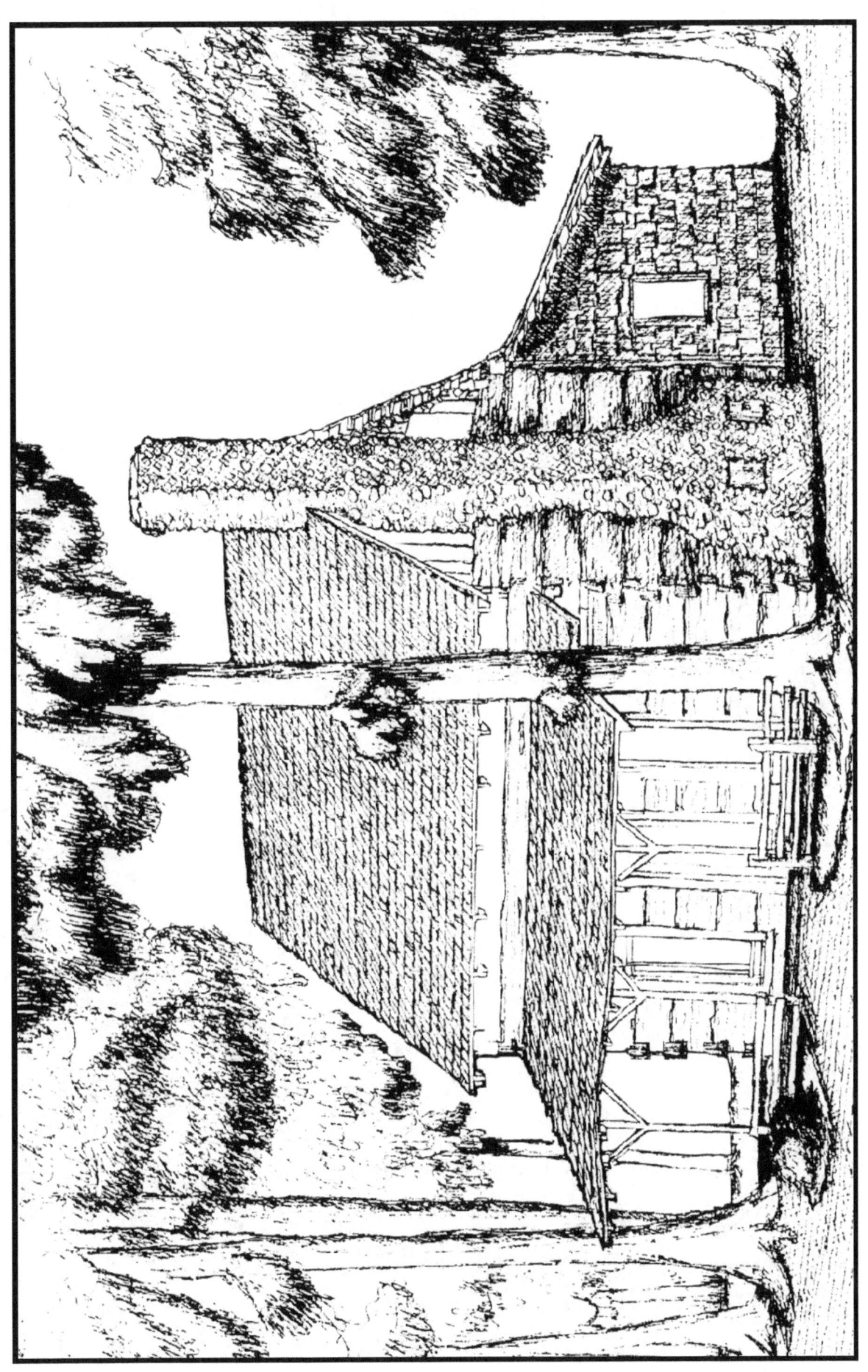

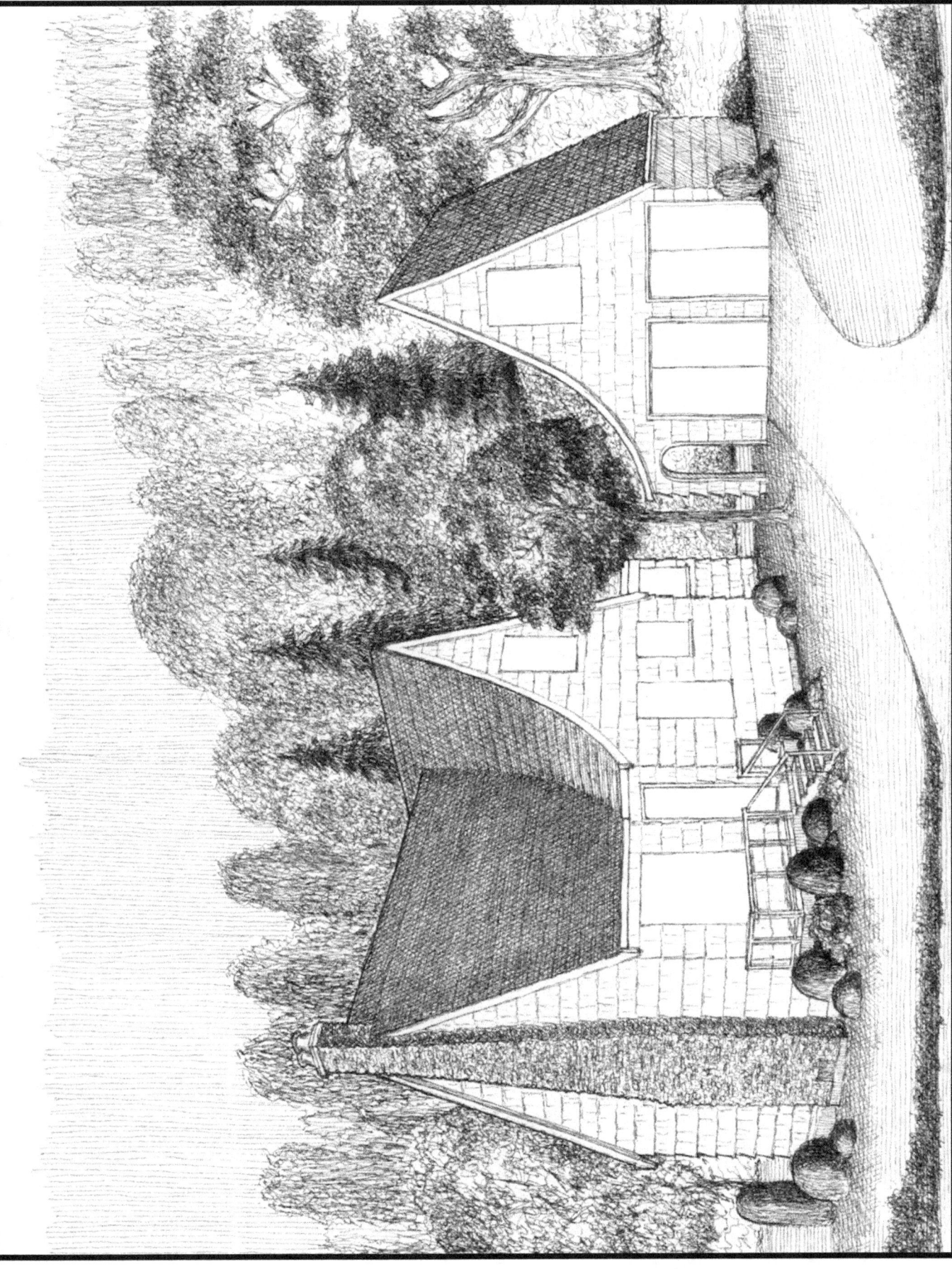

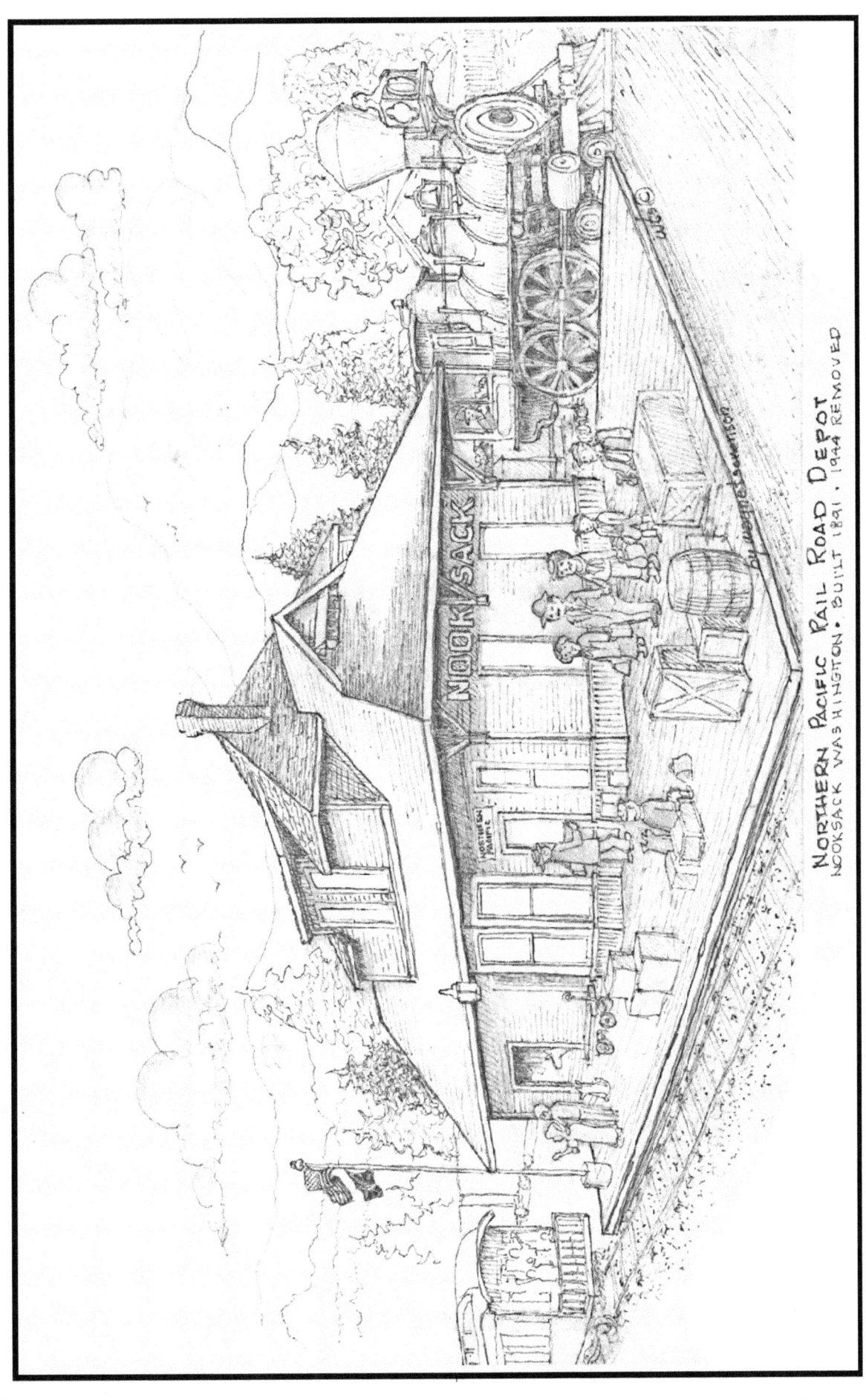

NORTHERN PACIFIC RAIL ROAD DEPOT
NOOKSACK WASHINGTON · BUILT 1891 · 1944 REMOVED

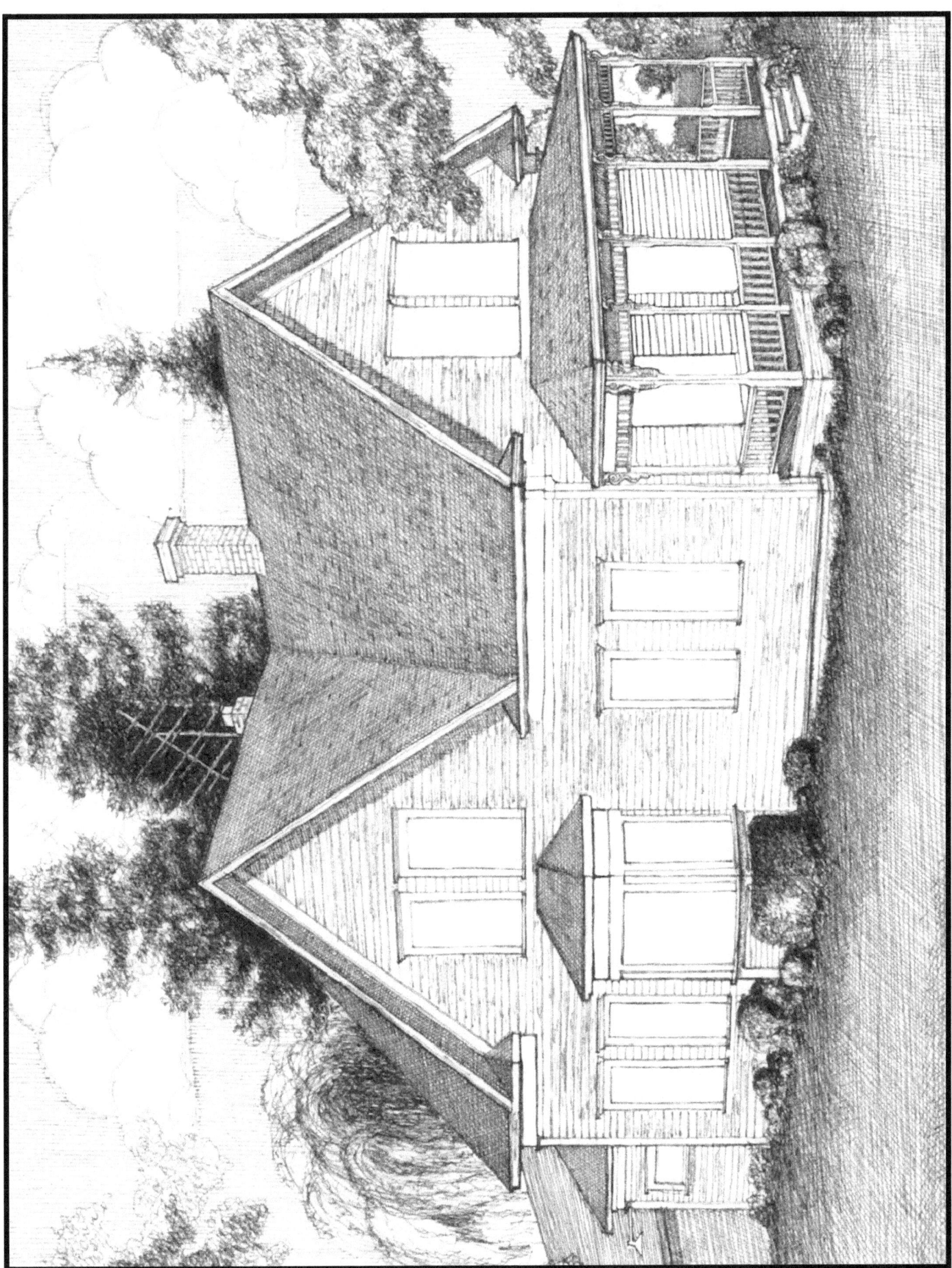

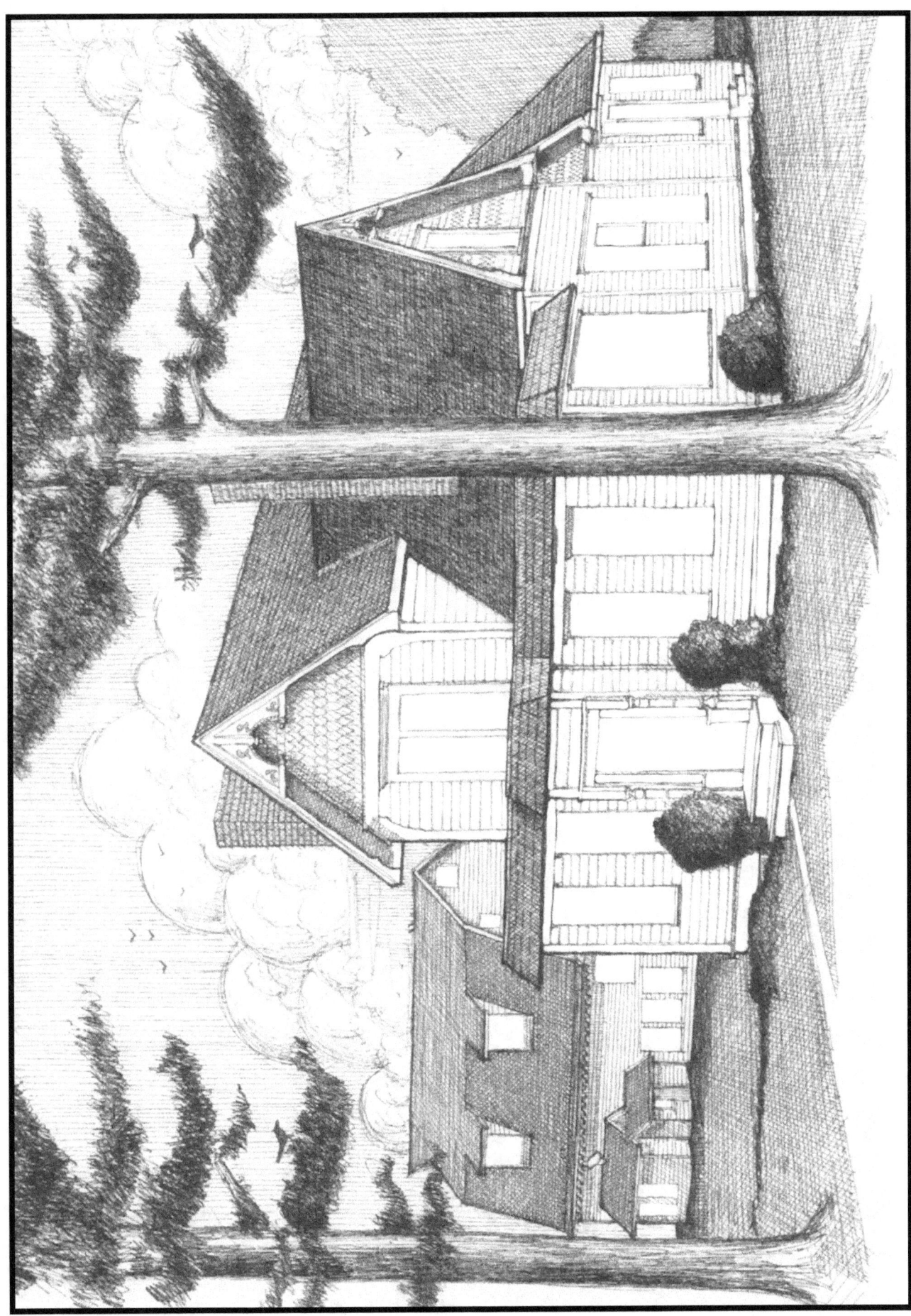

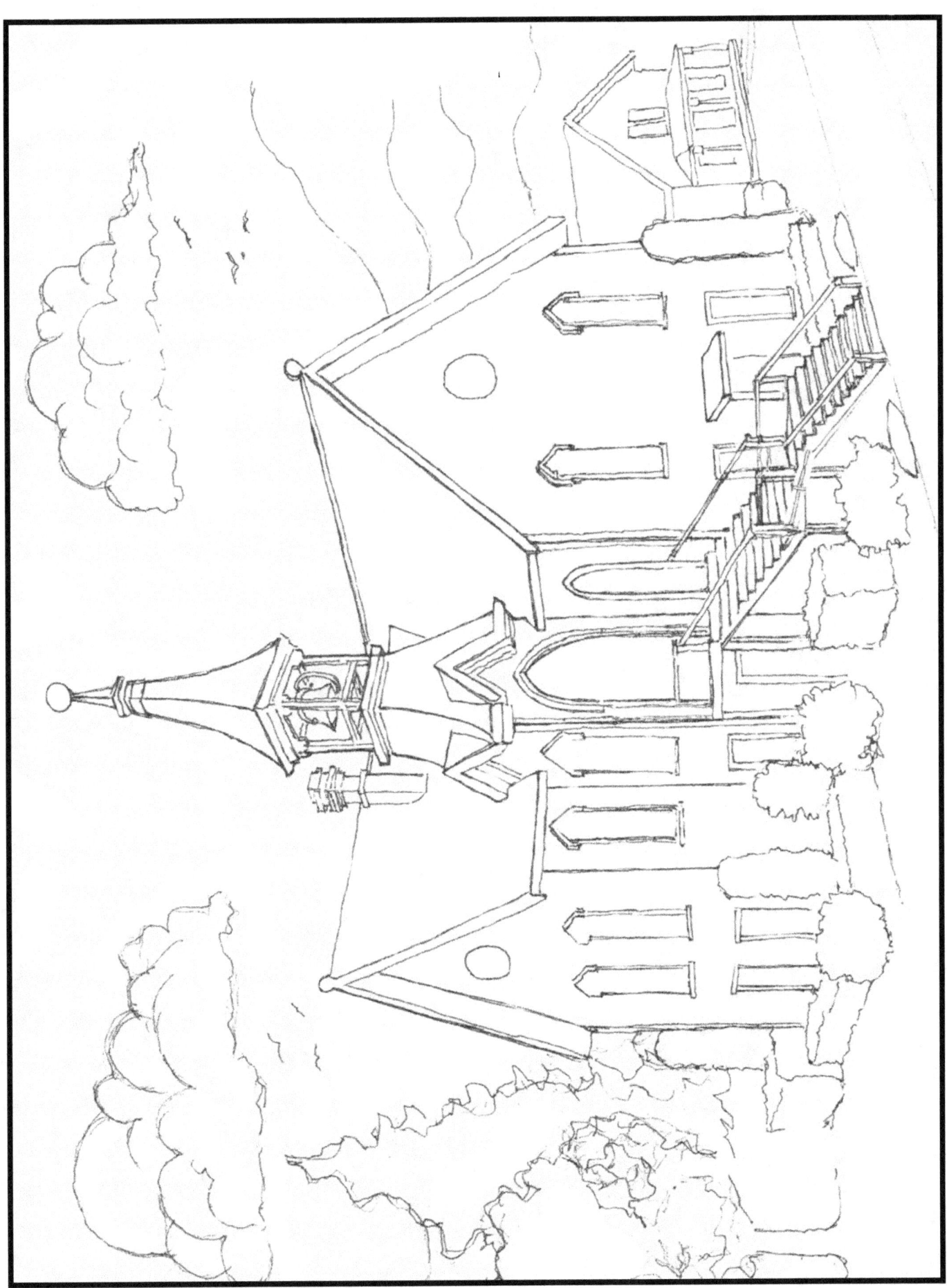

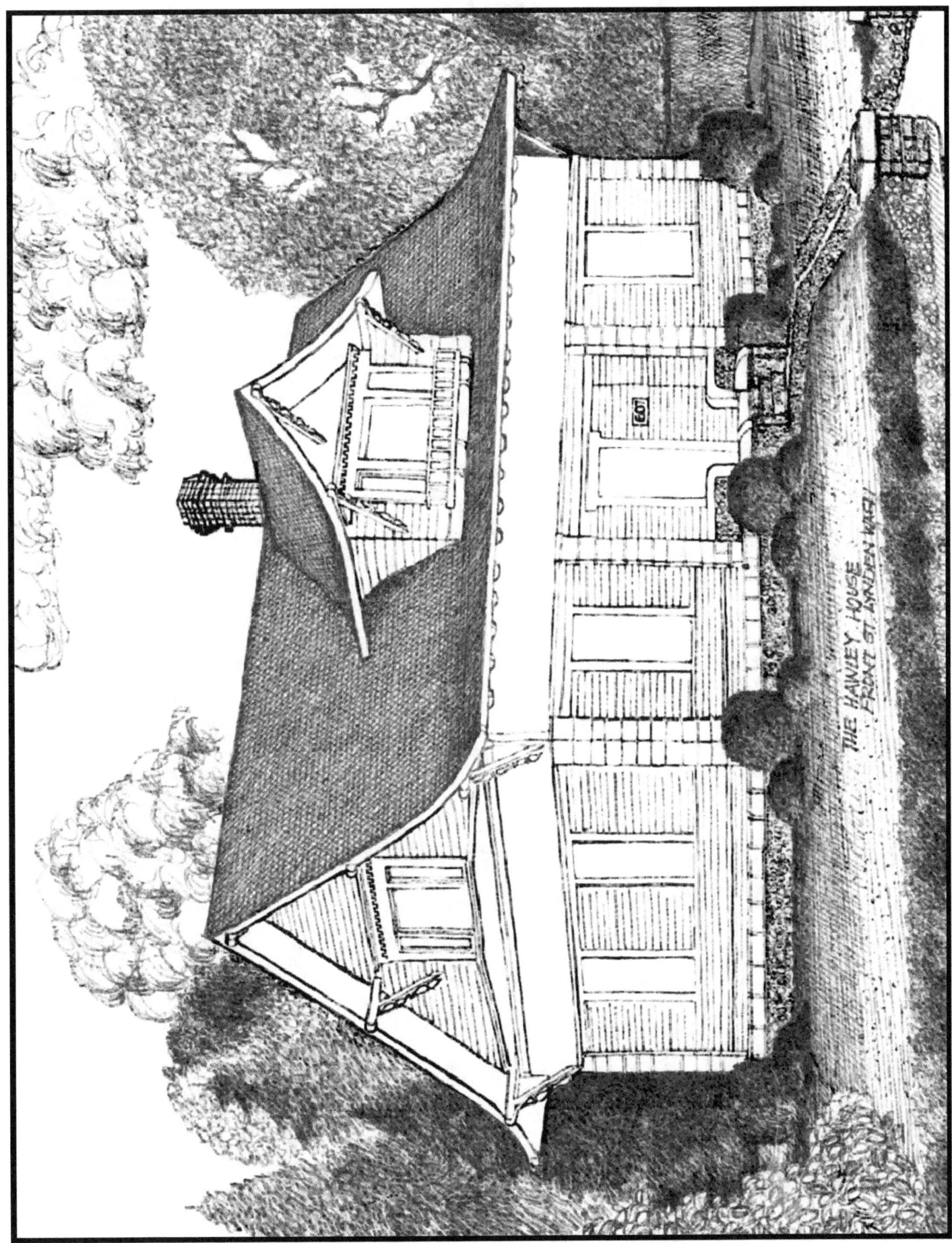

THE HAWLEY HOUSE
FRONT ST. LYNDEN WASH.

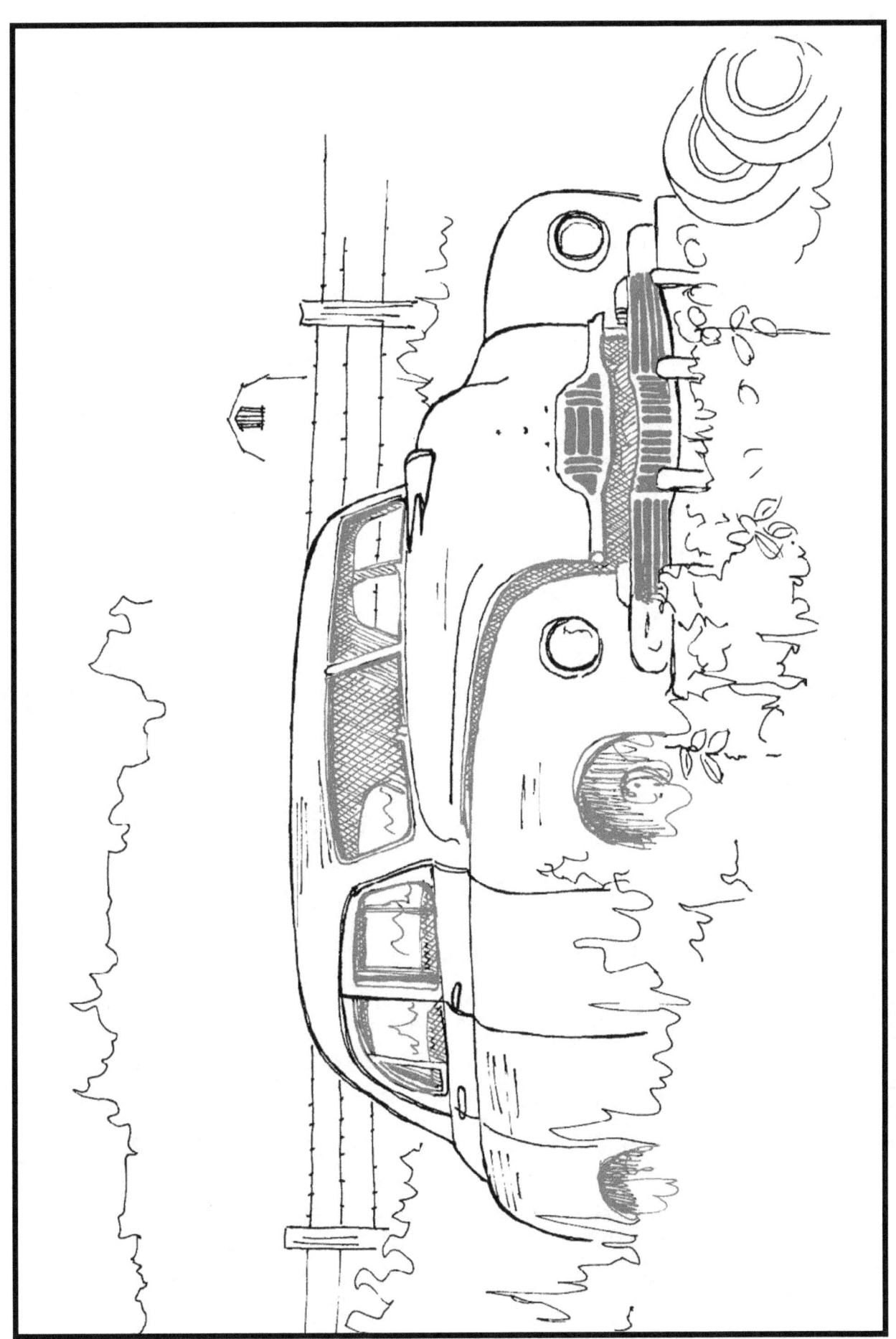

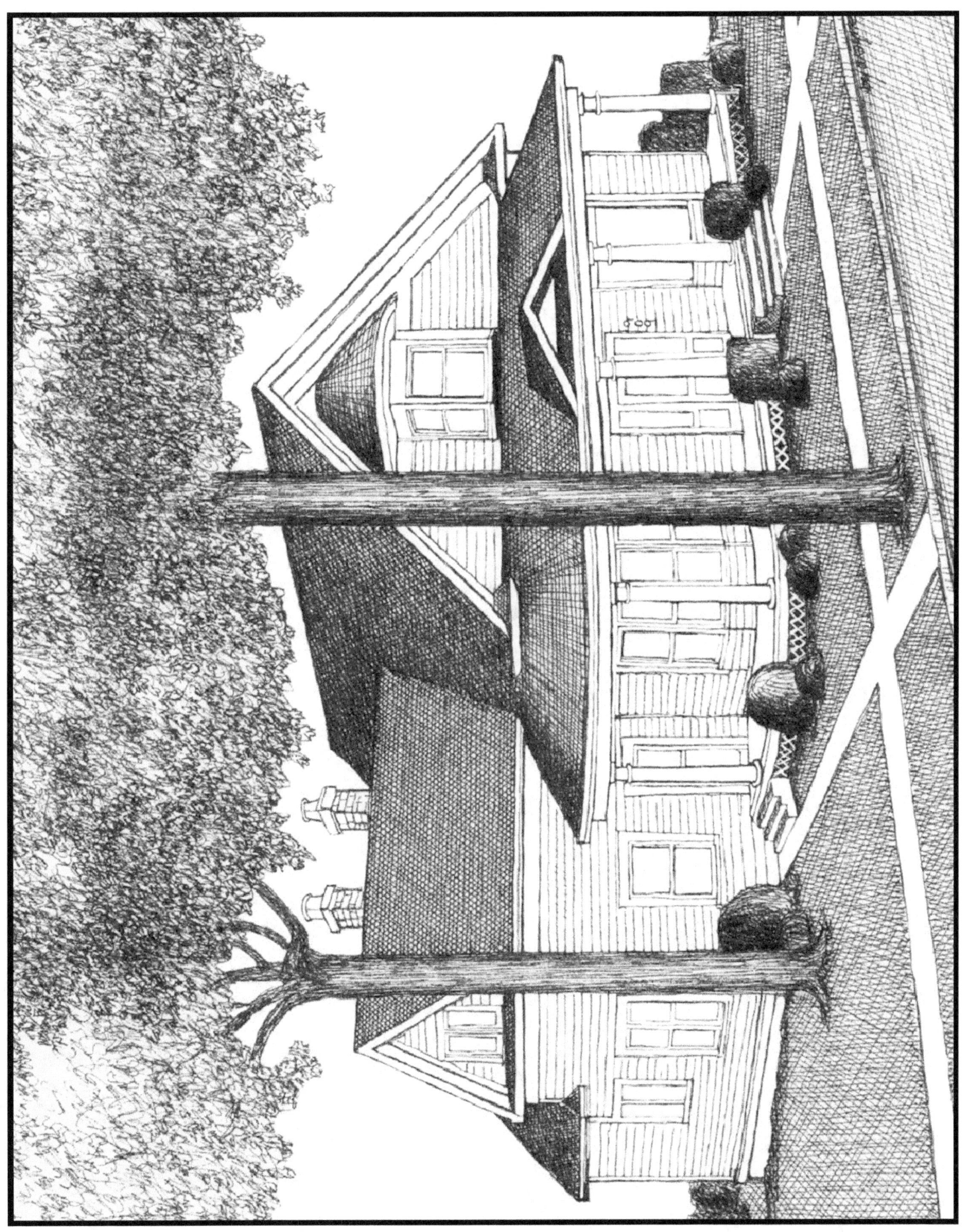

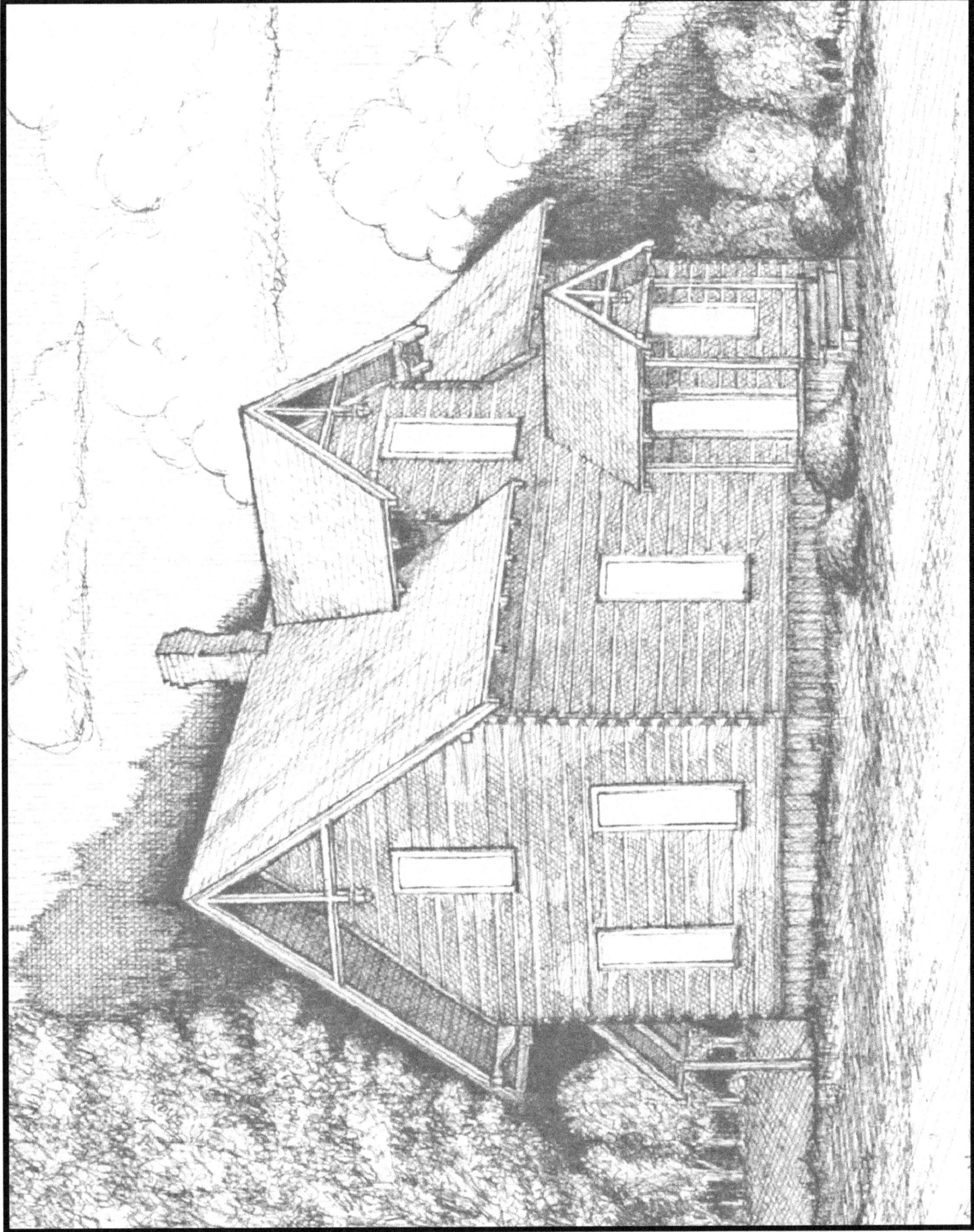

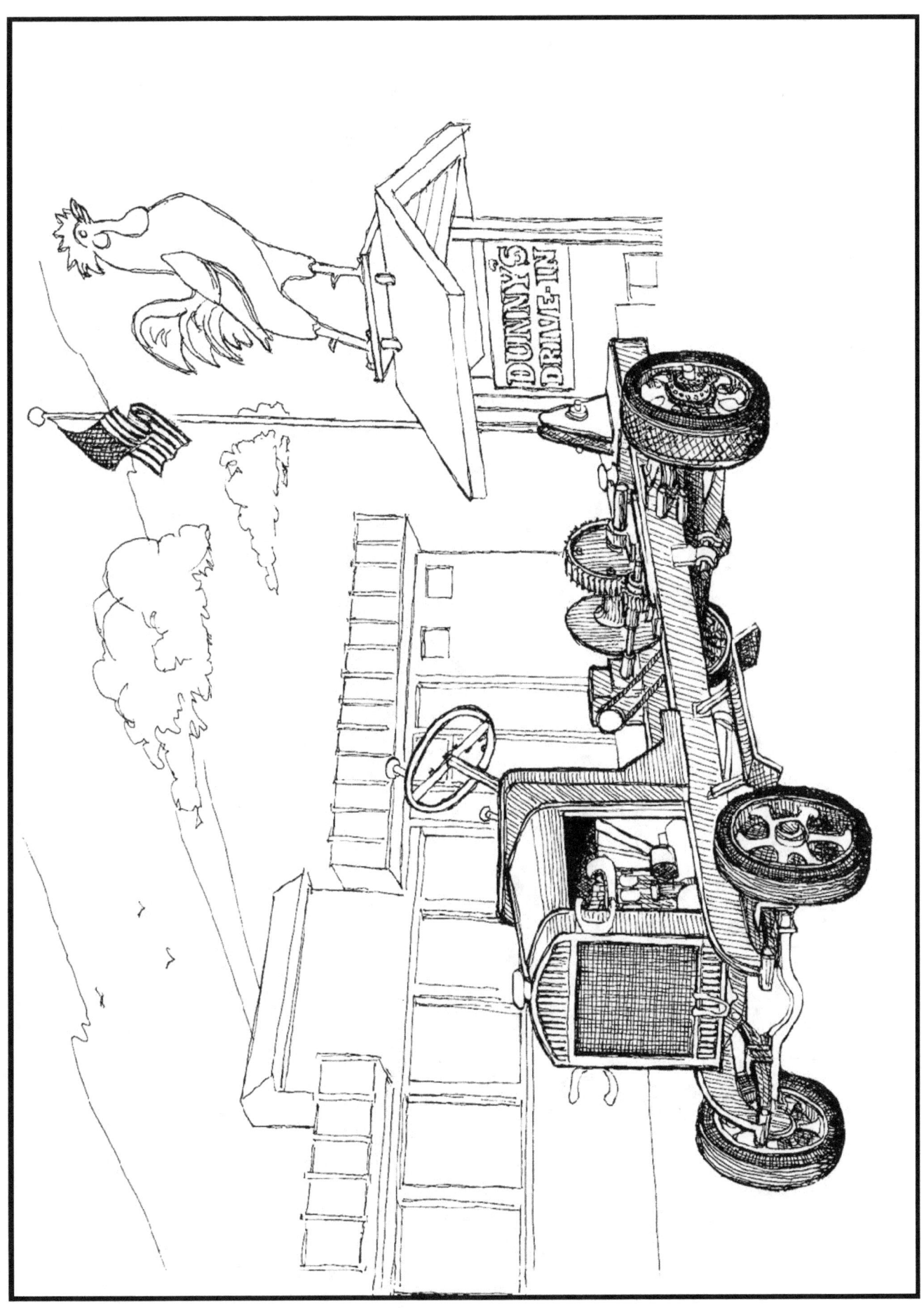

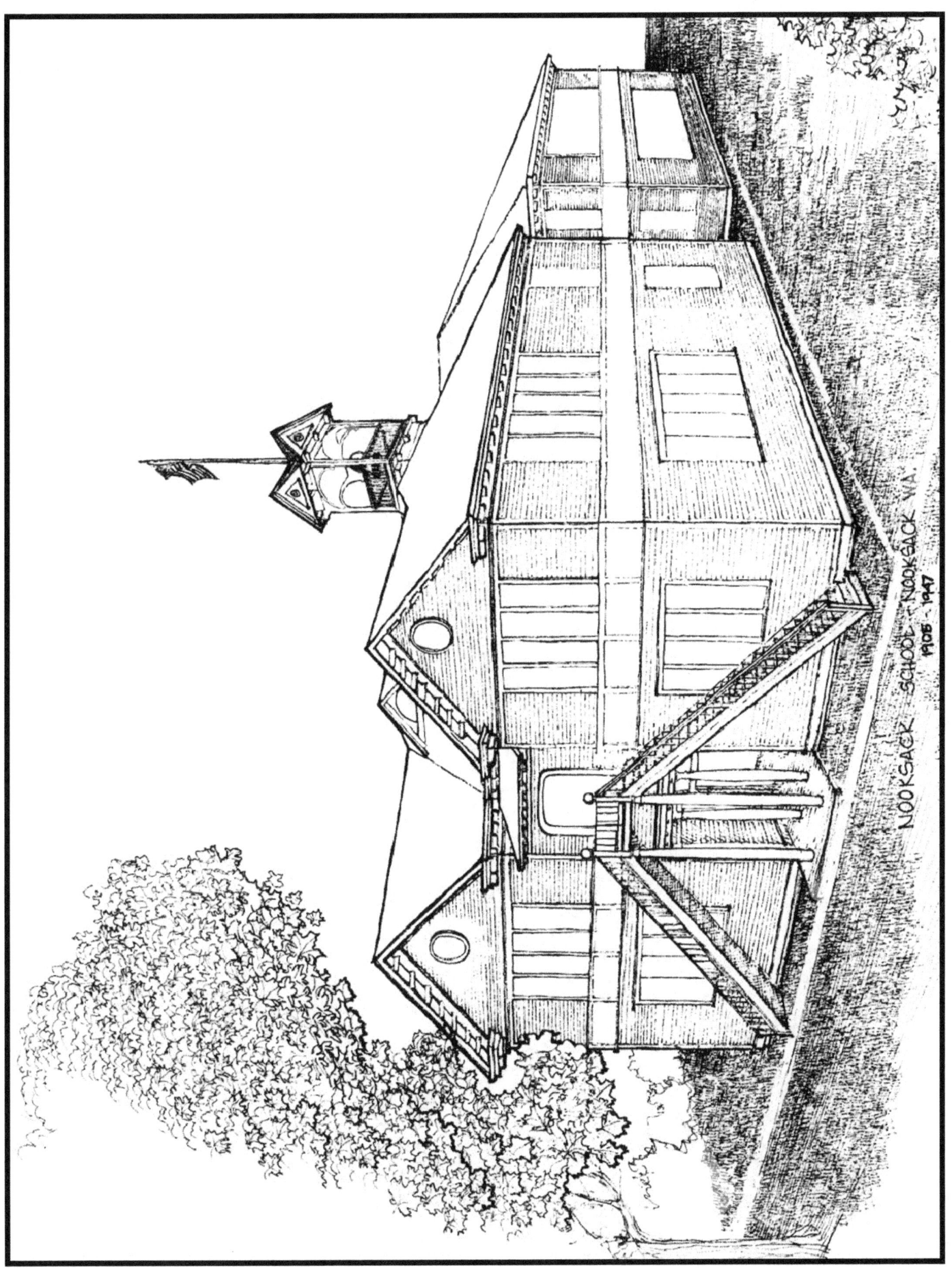

NOOKSACK SCHOOL ~ NOOKSACK WA.
1905 - 1947

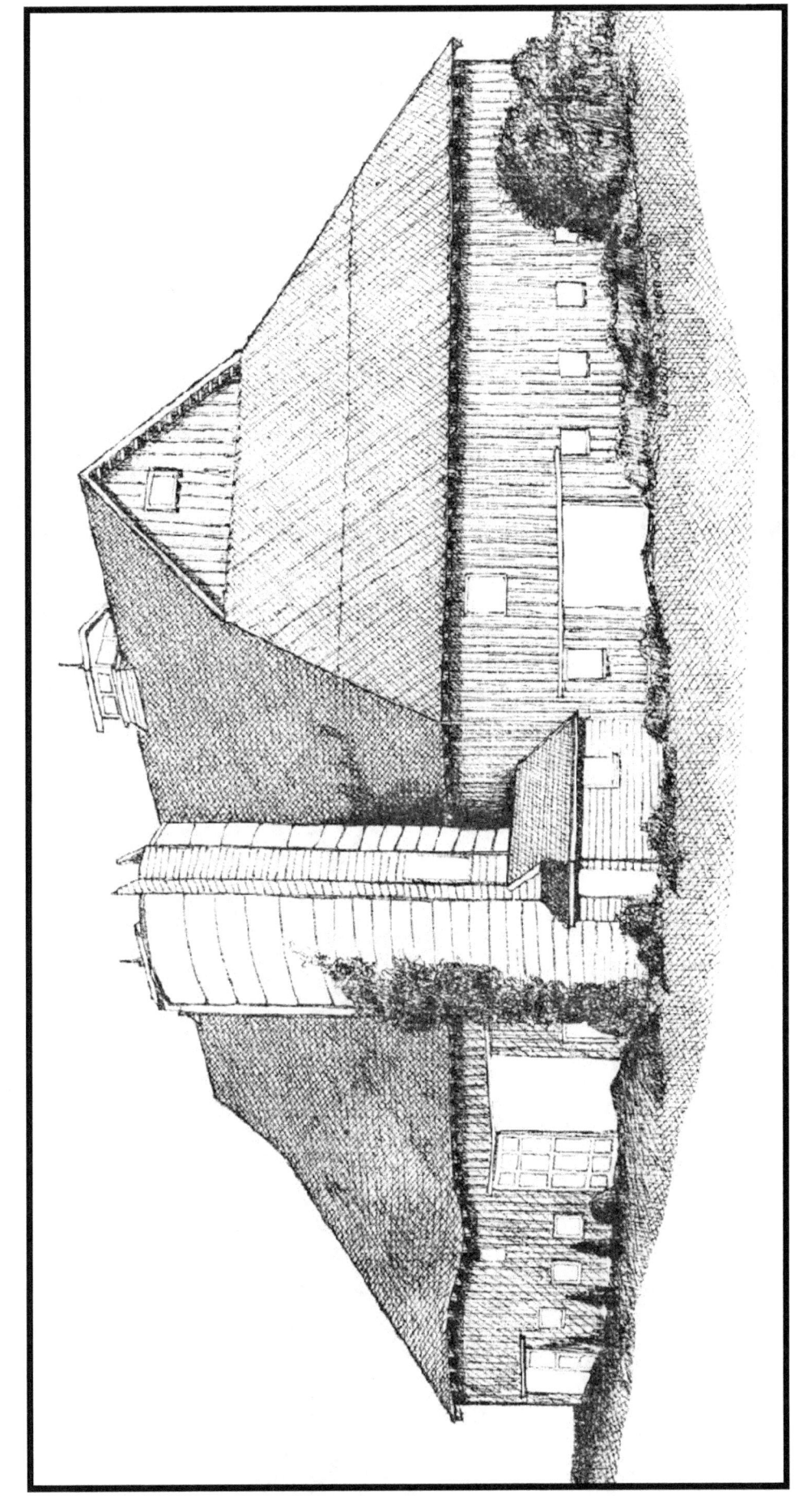

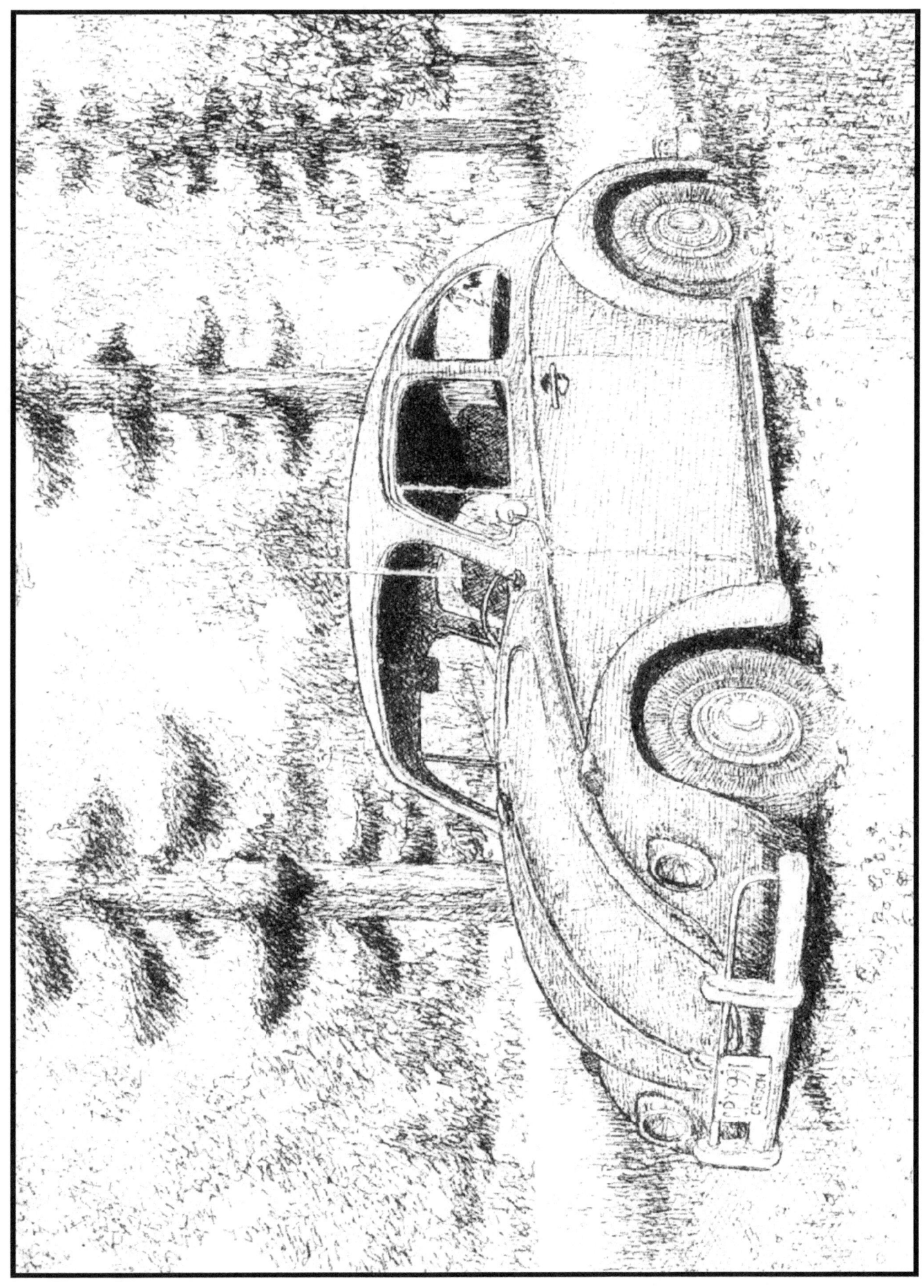

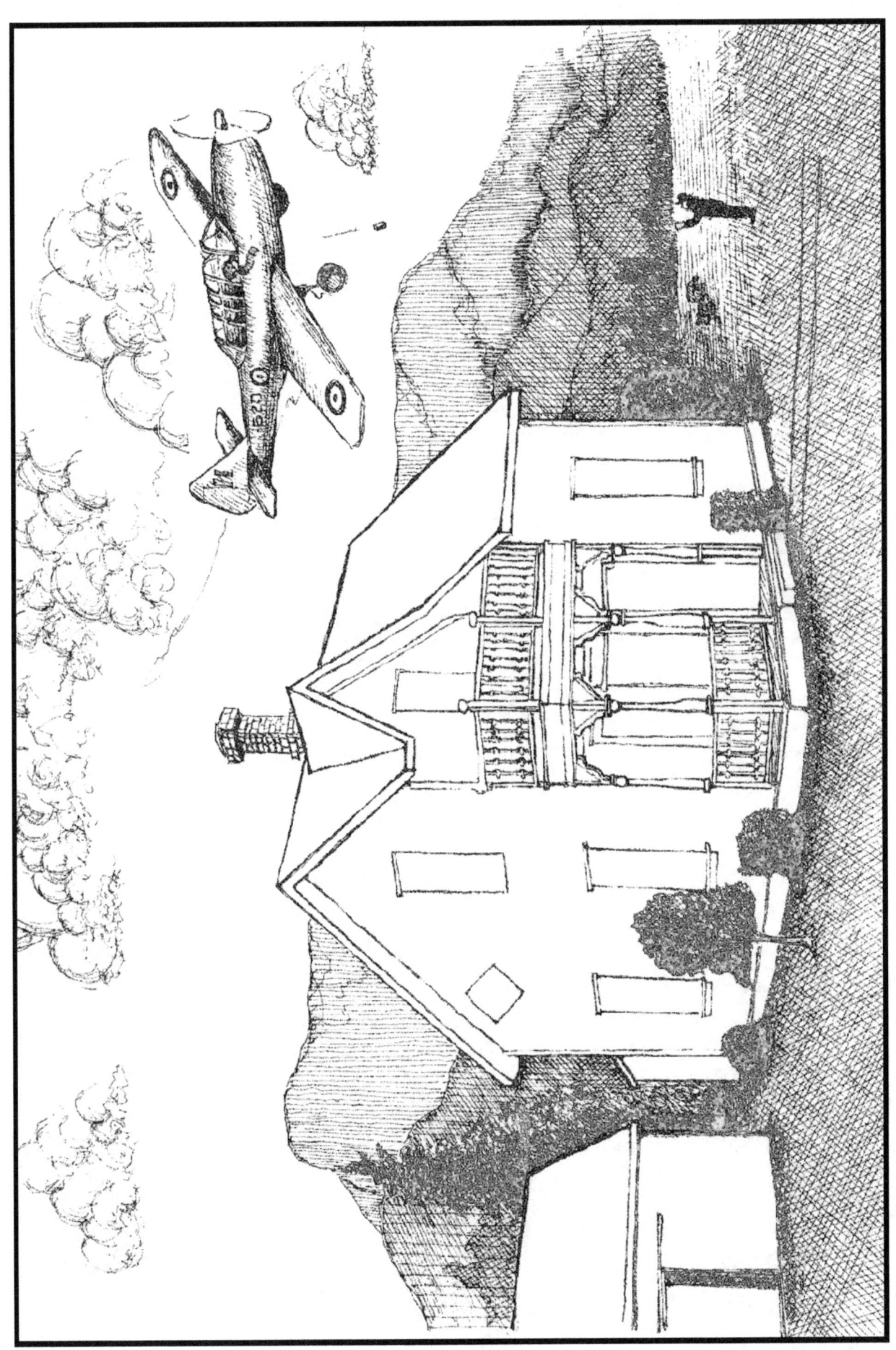

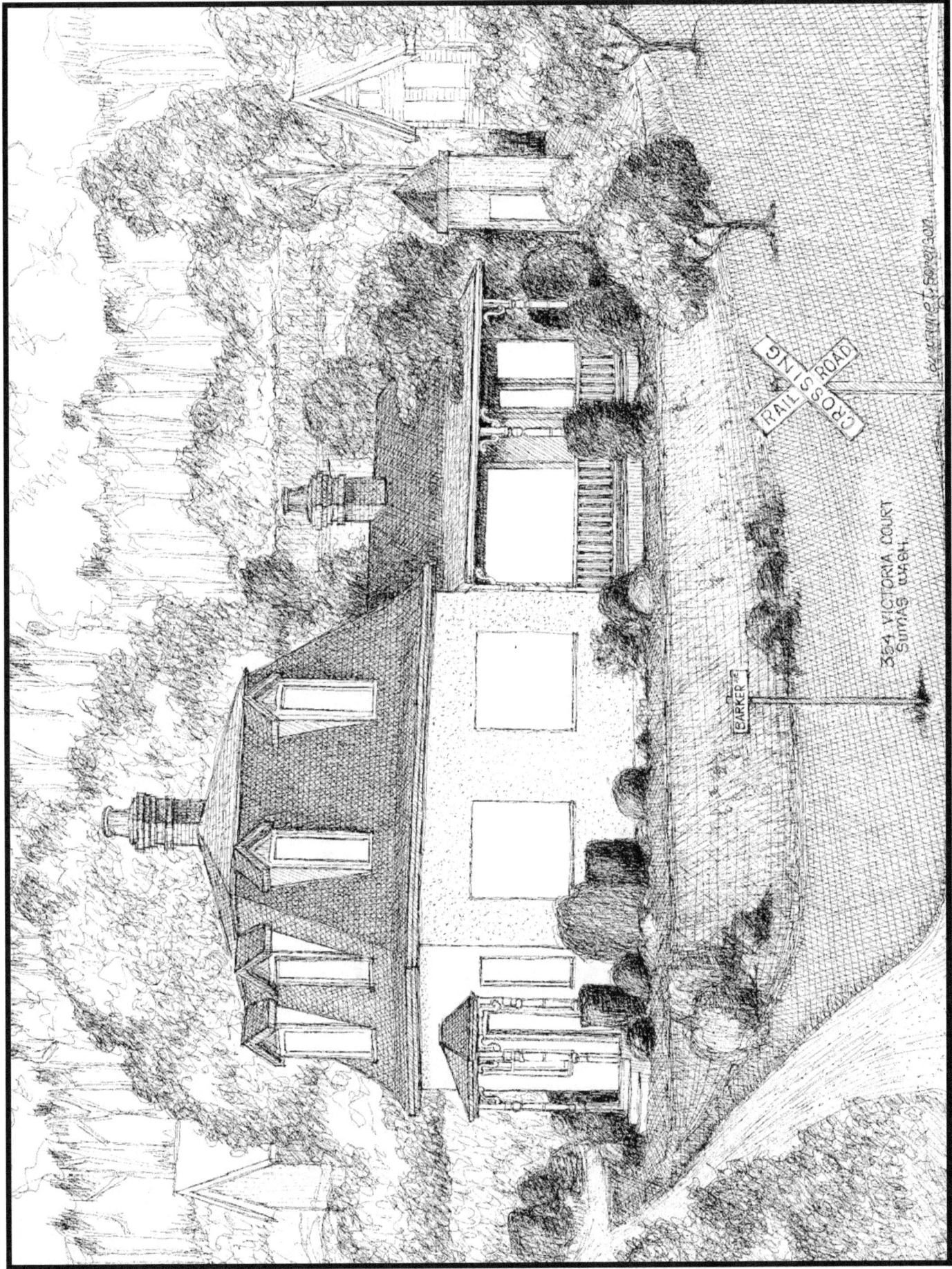

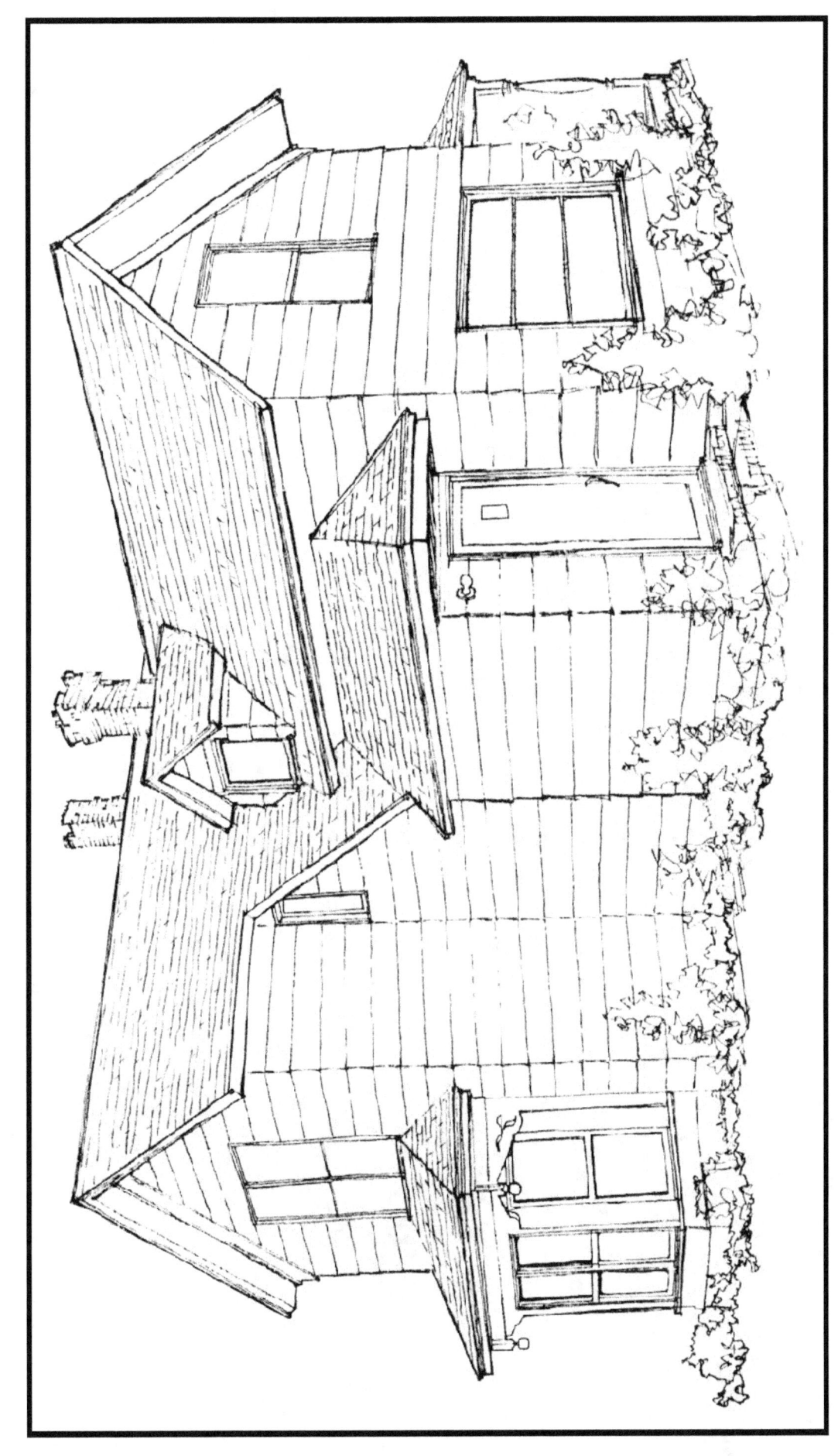

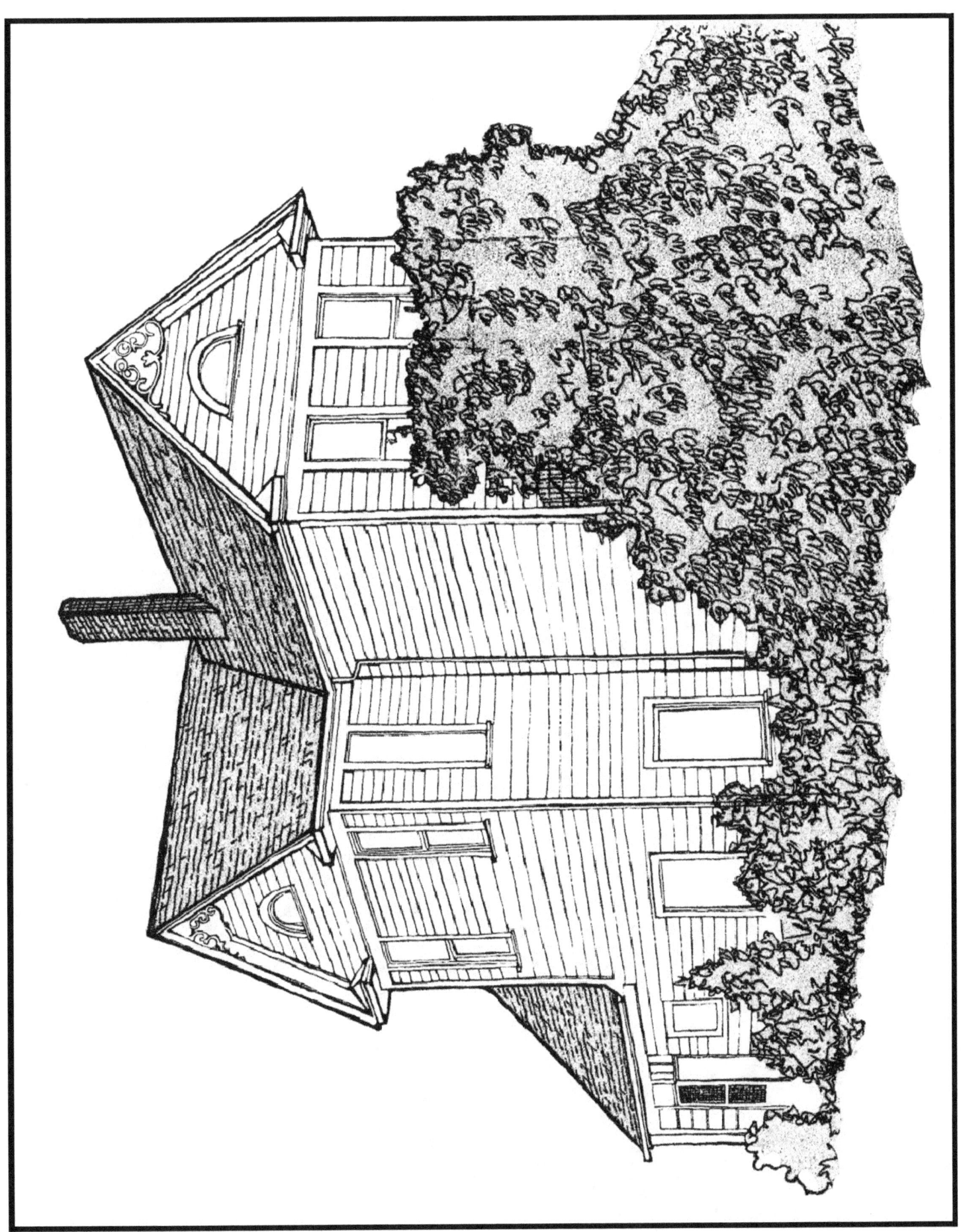

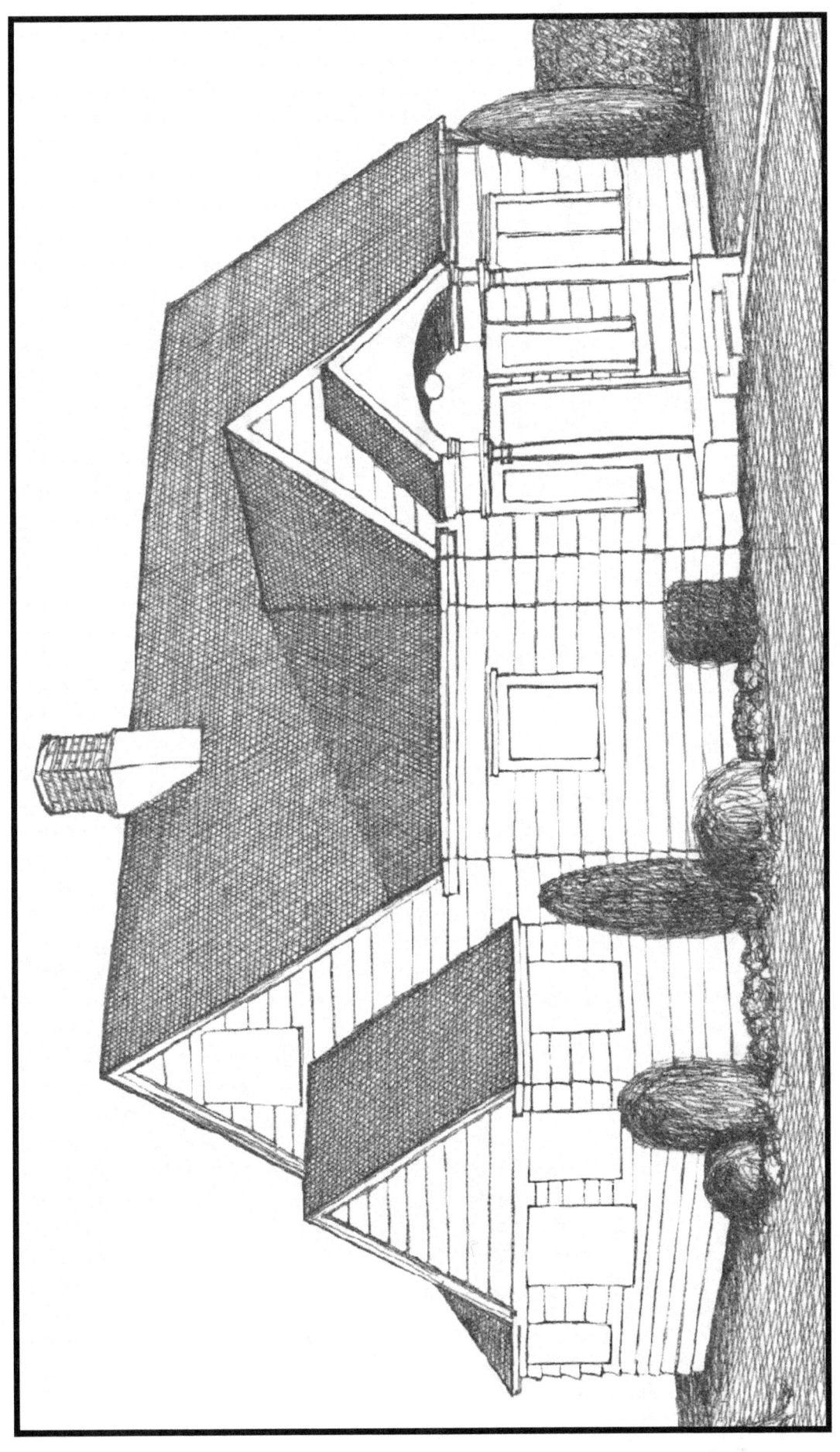

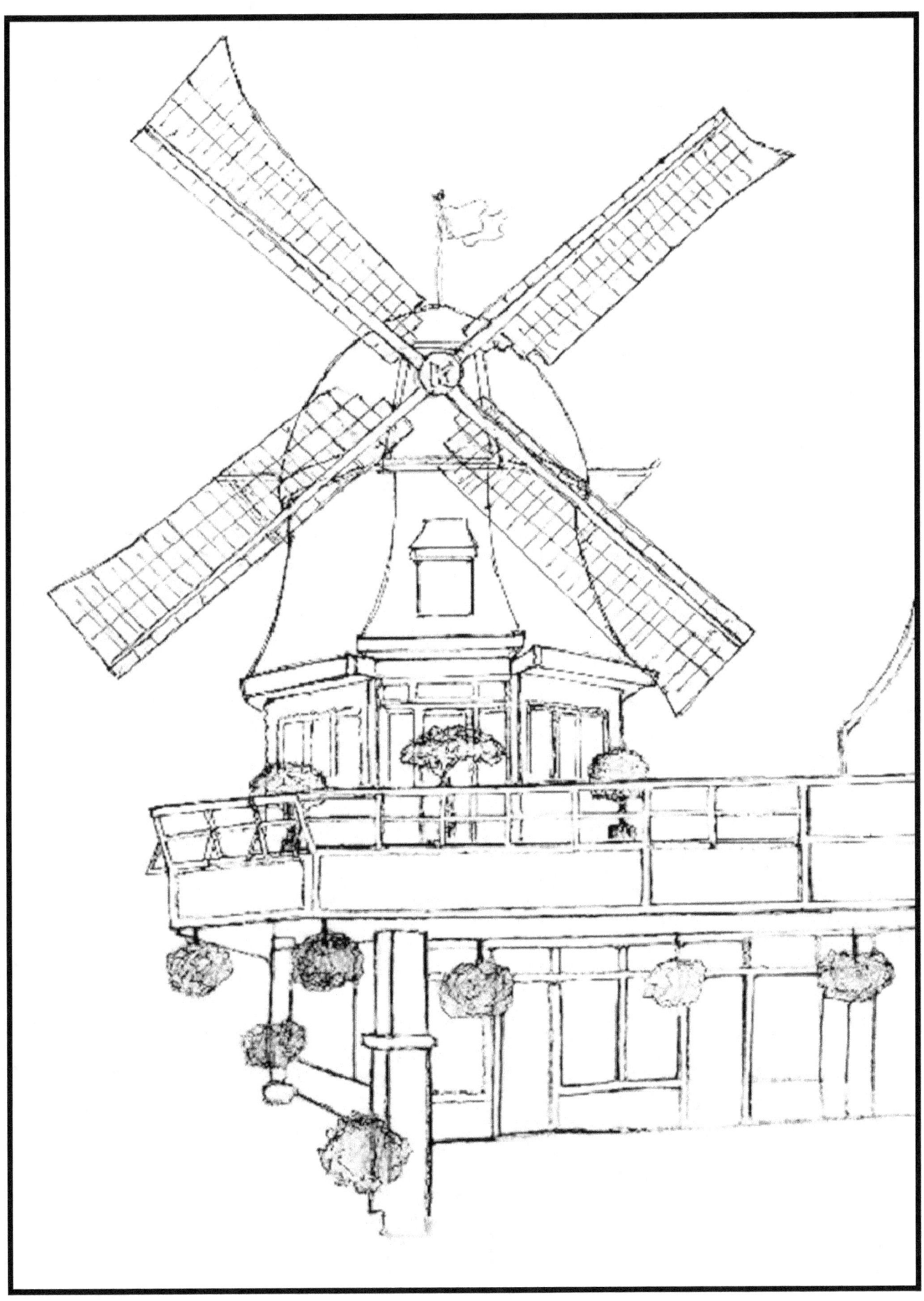

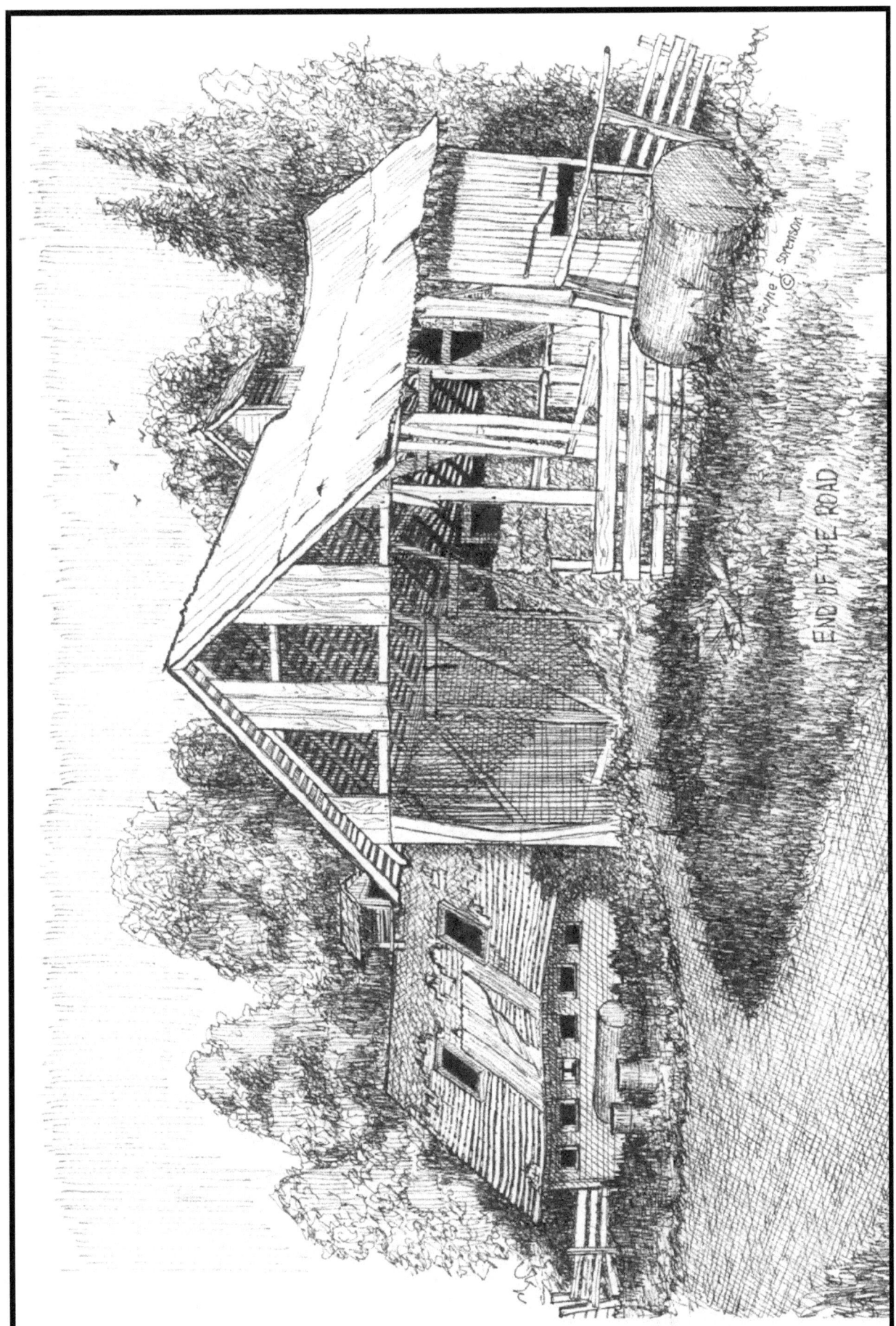

END OF THE ROAD.

Please Stay in Touch

If you liked this coloring book, please leave us a review.

Like us on Facebook or Instagram
In My Father's House

and post your favorite colored pages - we would love to
see what you have done to make them your own.

The End